Praise for *A Cry from the Womb:*

"This is an intriguing, thought provoking and important work, and surely a cry from the heart of the author to the heart of a reader.

Gwendolyn Jones' extensive knowledge of and keen analysis of conception, the uterine state, birth, bonding and general development is right on target, giving fresh insights into issues of profound importance to our present perilous state.

Her plea that the pre-conceptual period be a time of preparation <u>for</u> conception, a preparation which can bring into the world a new human of greater intelligence and ability, is backed by strong research and striking examples of which I have personal acquaintance.

Her stand on abortion is free of the political religious power-seeking abuse currently muddying the waters of that painful subject, introducing an aspect which I had never heard nor thought of; while her general guidance for unwanted pregnancy is compassionate, intelligent, and helpful.

Above all, this is a book about the plight of children and the human spirit in general, as well as the spirit children bring into the world with them, (as explored by psychologist Tobin Hart in his remarkable work, *The Secret Spiritual World of Children),* a spirit which is too often crushed by our insensitivity to an infant-child's real needs.

At this time of social disintegration, with its mounting rise of child suicide and violence, there is an equally strong social hunger for spiritual renewal, and to both Gwendolyn Jones brings an important, and challenging, viewpoint and message."

JOSEPH CHILTON PEARCE Author of *The Biology of Transcendence: A Blueprint of the Human Spirit; The Crack in the Cosmic Egg; Magical Child and Evolution's End.*

A CRY
FROM THE WOMB

ALSO BY GWENDOLYN AWEN JONES

The Angels' Guide Book to Living on Earth

The Angels' Guide to Forgiveness

A CRY
FROM THE WOMB

HEALING THE HEART OF THE WORLD

A guide to healing and helping Souls return to the Light
after sudden death, miscarriage, stillbirth or abortion

Gwendolyn Awen Jones

A Cry from the Womb
Healing the Heart of the World

A guide to healing and helping Souls return to the Light
after sudden death, miscarriage, stillbirth or abortion

by Gwendolyn Awen Jones

1st paperback edition

Published by:
Angels of Light and Healing
P.O. Box 311448 New Braunfels Texas 78131-1448 USA
www.angelsoflightandhealing.org

Originally published as a Deluxe Limited Edition of 1,000 copies
by Angels of Light and Healing in 2004

Cover and book design by Gwendolyn Awen Jones

Publisher's Cataloging-in-Publication Data
Jones, Gwendolyn Awen.
A Cry from the Womb - Healing the Heart of the World: A guide to healing and
helping souls return to the light after sudden death miscarriage, stillbirth or
abortion / by Gwendolyn Awen Jones.
-- 1st paperback ed.
p. cm
Includes bibliographical references.
LCCN 2004099451
ISBN: Paperback edition: 0-9740730-1-6
ISBN: Deluxe limited edition: 0-9740730-0-8
1. Soul.   2. Spiritualism.   3. Children-Death-Psychological aspects.
4. Fetus--Religious aspects.   5. Bereavement--Psychological aspects.   1. Title
BF1275.S55J66 2004   133.9   QB104-800133

Printed in the United States of America

to the Souls of all children

About the Author

Gwendolyn Awen Jones lectures and works internationally as a medical intuitive, Spiritual teacher and healer. Her work has helped bring a sense of peace and healing to numerous clients. Over the years, Gwendolyn has seen a pattern of illness in many of her clients relating to the loss of a child. Many of these client case histories are discussed in this book. It is her deepest desire that the lost Souls of children and all Souls who have been left behind reach the Light, so that all families may heal their hearts. As their hearts heal, so does the Heart of the World.

Acknowledgements

Many of my clients encouraged me to write this book as a guide to help others. Some of their stories are included here, and I am grateful to them for allowing me to write about their experiences. Yet, for all their prompting, this book was not an easy one to write because I knew I would be cutting through so many well-established beliefs and points of view. For four years I struggled with how to approach it. I wrote and rewrote several versions. Finally, I simply knew that I had to tell my own story in my own words and let the words fall where they may. I have endeavored to explain how I reached my understanding of the complicated realms of the Spiritual world, and I sincerely hope that you will be able to read this book with an open mind and heart.

When I struggled with the idea of facing great opposition to my book, it was Mother Mary who came to me and said, *"For every opposing voice there will be ten thousand Angels on your side."* I thank God for Mary. This truly is her book. Every child's Soul that has reached the Light in my sessions has been held in her arms for healing. Without Mary's loving assurance, and the help of Christ, my teams of Angels and all my guides and teachers, none of this work would have been done.

I also want to thank all my readers, friends, clients and my family for their loving support.

God is with us all,

Gwendolyn Awen Jones

A Cry From The Womb

Table of Contents

About the Author	viii
Acknowledgements	ix
Important Note	xv

INTRODUCTION   1

With an Open Heart, an Inquiring Mind
and with Wholeness of Spirit   3

PART I.

UNDERSTANDING SPIRITUAL VISION   5

Healing the Heart of the World	7
From Darkness into Light The Journey of my Soul	13
The Voice of the Unborn	27
Seeing Beyond the Physical Realm	31
The Higher Self	33
The Soul	33
The Mental Body	34
The Astral Body	35
The Emotional Body	36
The Etheric Body	37
The Physical Body	39
The Inner Child	40
The Chakras	41
Bringing in Higher Self	41

PART II.

CASE HISTORIES   43

The Rage of Mankind   46

The Tragic Miscarriage of an Abused Woman   52

The Sadness of Stillbirth   60

A New Child Brings Healing after a Stillbirth   70

Deep-Seated Fears of Sudden DeathTriggered by Son's Stillbirth   74

Why Could my Child Not Reach the Light?   80

Her Lost Brother's Spirit Wanted to be Her Son   85

Woman's Heart Problems Came From Her Grandmother's Desire
to Have Her Aborted   93

Did a Pregnant Young Woman's Suicide Attempt
Replay her Mother's Thoughts of Abortion?   97

Abortion Affects a Husband's Heart   100

A Century's Old Curse Behind Eight Abortions   105

Aversion to Pregnancy Comes from Past Life Death in Childbirth   111

When a Child Dies   118

Abortion after X-ray Exposure, a Child Returns Quickly   128

Talking With a Breech Baby's Spirit Before Birth   129

Was She the Child of Another Man?   132

An Adopted Child's Upset at her Birth Mother
Causes Cancer in Later Life   135

How the Death of an Unknown Birth Parent
Affects the Adopted Child   137

The Grief of a Mother Living in Fear of Being
Found by the Son She Gave up for Adoption   139

When the DNA Does Not Match, a Child Needs Truth   141

PART III.

HEALING THE WOUNDS   145

The Many Wounds of Childhood   147

The Lost Legions on the Inner Plane 153

Walk with the Angels in the Light 167

A Question of Choice 175

A Special Note to Doctors, Nurses, Healthcare
Workers and Counselors 193

A Special Note to All Women Who Have Had an Abortion 195

A Special Note to All Women Who Have Lost a Child 196

PART IV.

PRAYERS OF FORGIVENESS AND TRANSITION 197

THE SACRED RITES 199

The Prayer Work Begins 199

Opening the Sacred Space 200

The Prayer of Light 203

The Forgiveness Prayer 205

The Transitional Prayer 208

Closing the Time Doorways and the Sacred Space 210

PART V.

SUMMARY 213

Summary 215

AFTERWORD 221

Journey to the Moment of Conception 223

REFERENCE SECTION 227

GLOSSARY 233

OTHER BOOKS BY THE AUTHOR 239

✦

Important Note

If you have been through any situations similar to those described in these stories, please know that the prayers at the back of this book can help you. Much of the information in this book will be new to most people, and it may come as a shock. Individuals cannot be held responsible for what they did not know or understand. Forgiving yourself and others is essential for you, your family and your lost child's Soul to heal. Be at peace and know that the Angels are with you now as you read this book.

✦

Introduction

With an Open Heart, an Inquiring Mind and with Wholeness of Spirit

It is my desire in this book to give you tools to heal yourself and any lost Souls of your children. It is my wish that you may be free of any sadness and that you may find joy and wholeness in your life again.

It is not my intention to espouse any one way of seeing the world, nor to suggest that you change any religious or non-religious views you may have. I am here only to tell you the truth as I have found it, through my work as a medical intuitive and healer.

I believe there is one basic Energy or Source throughout the universe that lies behind all things. No matter what we call that Energy, we are all connected to it. However, disruptive thoughts such as grief or anger at ourselves, or another, can cut us off from fully being at One with that connection, causing us to become ill.

This book is the culmination of many years of research into the non-physical realities behind illness after the loss of a child, no matter when or how the death occurred. I have focused particularly on the Souls of children who have died before, or during the birth process, as it is often they who have not had the full transitional rites done for them. Therefore, the grief is often hidden and has not been dealt with. The grief of the parents can stop the Soul of the child from leaving, as it binds the child to them with their emotional cords. This binding of energy often causes illness, particularly in the mother, but can also greatly affect the father of the child.

If you will read this information with an open heart and inquiring mind, it may change your life. Once you understand the principles operating behind all physical manifestation, you can make new choices on how you wish to live. I have included the prayers that I use for the necessary closures with the lost Soul. I have also explained all the steps for the transition of the Soul so that you may help your lost child reach the Light. These same prayers can be used for any other deceased family member that needs help.

If you will take the time to understand this work and help your child's Soul return to the Source, it may help you heal many wounds in your Being, and it may also help bring healing to all members of your family.

PART I.

UNDERSTANDING SPIRITUAL VISION

Healing the Heart of the World

I am a medical intuitive and have the ability to see all levels of human consciousness. I have the equivalent of X-ray vision, and I am able to scan through all the levels of the human body through to the DNA. I am also able to travel to distant times in order to reach lost aspects of a person's Soul on the inner plane, and I work with teams of Angels, Christ and Mother Mary to bring healing to those who seek my help.

People come to me for healing after learning of my work by word of mouth. Whether they are atheists, agnostics or believers in one of the great religions, clients come to me because they know that what I do works. It is a gentle and loving healing process that brings peace and grace to the Souls of my clients, reuniting them with their Sacred purpose. The reason I am now writing this book is that there are many individuals I cannot see as clients who may benefit from what I have to teach, and hopefully they will find methods for their own healing process in these pages.

My healing work began from my own need to be healed. My training began with a family of healers or "curanderos," who were called "Meztizos," as they had the mixed blood of the Spanish and native Indians in Mexico. This family was Catholic by faith, of Mayan descent, and used an ancient Mayan system of healing. The mother used herbs and prayers and taught me how to use my natural gift of Spiritual sight. The father was a trained MD and spoke five languages fluently. Their son, a natural healer, was a year younger than I. The father had chosen to live in the back streets of Mexico City in order to serve the poor. I was twenty-three when I met them, visiting from England with no understanding of this kind of healing work; however, I was very ill at the time, and I was desperate to try anything. After the mother healed me, she told me that Christ, Mary and the Angels were blessing me and saying I was destined to become a healer myself. I told her I was dubious that they existed and that I had given up on the church at age sixteen. Yet, even though I was not a believer, the pain in my belly that had been with me for a year and a half miraculously disappeared.

✦

I resisted the idea of being a healer for many years, as I was a photographer and illustrator, with a Dip.A.D. (a degree equivalent) from England in visual communication. I had no desire to have a healing practice with many people at my door. I was simply not ready. However, over the years I was drawn to study many levels of healing and Spiritual systems around the world. Ultimately, I came to my own understanding of the higher realms. It took me almost ten years to understand the depth of what the healer in Mexico and her family had taught me. It was not until I had created my own greeting card company and worked in special effects at Lucas Films in California that I finally had the calling to truly begin my life's work. I was thirty-nine at the time.

I left a good job, being trained to work on the same state-of-the-art computers that had recently been used to complete the highly acclaimed *Jurassic Park* movie, and I set out across the country to lecture and to begin my healing work. Since that time, I have counseled and helped many women and men in numerous places around the world. I use a combination of techniques, but they are all based upon that first experience with my Mayan friends. Like my first teacher, I work with Christ, Mary, the Angelic Kingdoms and with many Guides and Teachers from the realms of Light. I have the ability to see and hear the Spirit worlds, and it is this that allows me to access information about a client's condition that most doctors have missed. This is why clients come to me. Often they have a condition for which they have seen a doctor for years. I am able to look and see where this condition originated, and I can help them to process what they need in order to heal. Or, if I see that it is needed, I send them back to their doctor for a test on an area that I find has been missed. I am not a doctor, so I do not prescribe medications, although I do all that I can to educate my clients in the various herbals and remedies that are available. I have found tremendous power in herbs, homeopathics, flower remedies and essential oils for releasing conditions at the physical, emotional and Spiritual levels.

I also work with other practitioners to help them when they get stuck on a case. I can read long distance around the world, if necessary.

I have worked with many people from most religions. Often they come to me when they cannot find solace from their own particular teaching. As I studied the many Spiritual teachings from around the world, I found that, although the words might be different, the basic premise is the same. Most doctrines posit the idea of a central Creator, Being or Energy Source that is behind all creation. That Source or Creator has been named many things in many different languages, such as God, Goddess, Father-Mother-God and more. *God* is the term that is used most frequently, but the word *God* has been interpreted according to the dogma of so many different groups, that many people who have had a bad experience with one or another religious group are likely to have a negative reaction to the word *God*. Likewise, if convoluted and inaccurate versions of Christ, Mary or any other great teacher have been given to people, they may have a poor response to these names as well.

It took me years to come to terms with these names after the confused teachings I had received in my childhood from well-meaning people in the local Church of England.[1] Deep down I felt there was a greater Being than myself, but I would not use the word *God* for many years after I left the church, as I did not want to connect to a belief in the vengeful and wrathful God of the Old Testament. I felt the Source I believed in was above and beyond petty human emotions and that for centuries people had only been able to understand that Source through their own limited physical world-view. Likewise, I felt that the beautiful essential Beings of Christ and Mary and the Angels were also misunderstood and limited by the inevitable lack of perception of those bound by the Physical Body. Each Spiritual Being is so much more than what our physical senses can perceive.

I finally came to see that a Christed Being is one whose heart is fully conscious of, and fully illuminated by, the Divine Love of the Creator. This Divine Love, or Christ Light, over-lighted Jesus in the Physical Body. We can all choose to become Christed, or illuminated by Divine Love, through prayer work and a true desire to be at One with the loving heart of the Creator. I believe there are great teachers from all religions, currently living, who have attained this enlightenment through Divine Love.

---

[1] *Note: There are some wonderful Spiritual Teachers in the Church of England. I just did not find them until much later in life.*

9

I use the name *Christ* in this book to mean the Spiritual Master, Jesus, in His Christed Awareness. Jesus is still available in Spirit to us as a Guide and Teacher, and can act as a bridge to the Divine Heart of God for those who choose to work with Him.

Jesus taught that Love heals all things. For those who do not believe in Jesus, I ask them only to accept Love from the Creator. I accept that all Spiritual Teachers from the different religions are a part of the greater whole and willingly work with them, if it is what a client needs to feel at peace. For those who do not believe in a Creator, I ask only that they receive the Light of Love. Most of my clients can accept that. I usually find those who say they do not believe in God are actually very angry at a religious system that has taught fear of God as a method of control. Their inner Spirit rebels at this, or they may be angry with God for something they think He did not do. Perhaps they feel God abandoned them or a loved one in a time of need. Sometimes there is a pain that needs resolution in that person's Being, a grief, perhaps, that has to do with someone passing who was close or dear to them. Finding the cause of their anger or grief and putting it to rest will bring a peaceful reunion with their Source; then the healing can begin.

✦

My dedication is simply to help those who are willing and ready to reconnect to their own Source of Truth and Oneness with the Creator. I do not ask for a dedication to my way, or that my clients believe in any particular religion. I ask only that those seeking Truth be open to receive their own Highest Truth from their own Source.

For simplicity in this book, I refer to the Creator as God or He, but in reality I feel that the Divine Source of all Creation is neither male nor female but is beyond the definition of gender. I refer to the healing principle from the Creator as Christ Light, which, I believe, is the highest form of Love. When Souls return to the Light, they are returning to the pure essential nature of the Creator, which is Love.

As many Spiritual texts differ in the translation of certain words, I have included a glossary at the back of this book to help you understand the meaning of terms I have used. I have endeavored to explain the Spiritual worlds as I see them, and this work represents my understanding of the Truth as I know it at this time. However, I am always reaching for deeper understanding of things as I progress on my journey. I keep an open mind and heart.

I include references to past lives, or reincarnation, in this book. Though some readers may feel that reincarnation is not a truth for them, it is something I have come to accept as a reality. Through all my years of work I have been able to see amazing historical detail in past lives and help heal clients by clearing the damage that occurred in those lives. This work most often relieves the painful physical conditions of my clients in this current life.

The concept of reincarnation was removed from the Bible in the fourth century A.D. by Emperor Constantine, who appears to have done so for political reasons and state control. Previously, in the ancient Christian Gnostic teachings and through early Christian writers such as St. Augustine, St. Clement, St. Gregory and St. Jerome, reincarnation was established as a reality. Most Eastern traditions hold the notion of reincarnation to be true.

✦

My desire in this book is to teach through stories, true stories with the names changed to protect my friends and clients. These stories are being shared with you to help you heal yourself and your loved ones. As your hearts heal, so does the Heart of the World.

✦

From Darkness into Light
The Journey of my Soul

A Soul must travel the path of its own creation in order to find the Source of Truth. Each of us has our own journey back to the Light of God. There are as many stumbling blocks as there are hands to help us. Inevitably the "dark night of the Soul" will arrive when we are tested to the fullest.

In these moments we may cry out to God and the Angels for help, if we know how to do this. Or, we may stumble blindly along, until some gentle Soul reaches out to us with love and compassion to help us on our way.

So it was for me. My journey was at times most difficult to comprehend, but always, with hindsight, I see I had choices each step of the way. I could have chosen differently, but what I chose made me who I am now, able to help others with compassion, as I have walked through many difficult places, places where many would prefer not to go. This has given me the strength to do the work I do, and the courage to help others face what they must do in order to find balance and peace in their own Souls.

✦

This, then, is my story. I offer it so you will understand how I came to do the work I do, and to light a path to healing for those of you who need to heal. It is not an easy story to read, but there is beauty in it and a teaching that may help you on your path toward wholeness. I urge you to persevere as I did and you will find the healing you seek.

I was born in North Yorkshire, England, near the cold North East coast, and I was brought up in fairly typical English fashion. My parents were schoolteachers and musicians. My father was the organist at the local Church of England, where I was baptized and confirmed. I sang with my two brothers in the choir every Sunday. I had a general belief system based on the stories of Christ, but I had also a "gift" that at the time disturbed me. I was able to see things that others did not see. It was called an "active imagination" until I began to speak of things from my visions that proved to be accurate predictions in the future. This made a lot of people uncomfortable, so over time I learned not to speak of what I saw; however, I did not know how to switch off the visions.

My father died of a heart condition when I was sixteen. The church could not answer my questions about life, death and the Spiritual Body of man. What happened to the body? Where did it go? Was there life after death? What did the church really understand of these things? I got no answers that made sense to me, and so I began to question the validity of everything I had been taught to believe. I wanted to know more. At that time my dreams and visions became more and more lucid. Everything began to shift for me dramatically.

A few weeks after my father's death, I was sitting quietly on my bed when I had a strange experience. I had no way of understanding what was happening, but suddenly I was floating above my body and looking down on it from the ceiling. I remember my confusion as I tried to figure out what was happening. *How could I be seeing me down there? What part of me was up here at ceiling level?* That shift of perception made me realize that there was an all-knowing, conscious part of myself that lives inside the physical body but is also separate from it. My physical body was still breathing all by itself sitting on the bed and looked normal. Then I got scared. Why was I out of my body? With that thought, I suddenly slipped back down towards the physical part of me and came back into my physical Being into the "me" I always thought I was. I was shocked and perplexed by this experience, yet it began to answer some questions. Could this be the Spirit part of myself that could even go beyond death? It began to make some sense.

Only a few months later an eighteen-year old friend of mine was killed on icy roads in a car wreck. His wife was in a coma, as a result of the wreck, leaving their small three-month old child with no one to care for her. I had sung in a rock band briefly the year before my father's death, and the young man who was killed had been a singer in one of the better-known bands in the area. All the rock groups decided to come together to raise funds for his wife and child. It was hard for me to accept the death of this young man who had everything to live for. My father had died at age forty-seven, but he had an illness that could not be cured. Somehow I could accept his death more easily. This young man was different. He was healthy and strong, and then suddenly he was gone through a tragic accident on black ice.

Again, I questioned the nature of death and a God that would allow this to happen.

After the memorial concert, I found myself thirteen miles from home with no ride back. My friends had all teamed up with new girlfriends, so the ride I thought I had no longer existed. An eighteen-year old boy I vaguely knew from school offered me a ride home. The weather had turned for the worse, and it was snowing outside when we left at midnight. I was dressed only in lightweight dance clothes, sandals and a short fur coat.

That night I was raped and left alone in the snow. It was a night I shall never forget, full of terror and cold. Shaking violently with the freezing cold, and numb with exhaustion, I eventually found a taxi after two hours walking in the snow. I had no money with me and prayed I would have enough to be able to pay the driver when I got home.

The roads were slick with ice, and the drive home was treacherous. I watched in dumb silence, shivering to the core, as the slow beat of the window wipers pushed the snow away from the windscreen. The orange yellow of the street lights blurred in streaks with each sweep. I felt like my life was ebbing away. I clung to consciousness, forcing myself to stay awake by digging my nails into my thighs. My clothes were wet through with the snow, and I felt filthy. Other than giving directions home, no words passed between the driver and myself. The fare cost me all the savings I had. All I knew to do was to get into a bath of hot water to save myself from hypothermia.

I had not called my mother, as she had houseguests, and I did not want to worry her at two o'clock in the morning. I knew better than to call the police, who were well-known for their lack of understanding and rough handling in rape cases.

As I sank into the hot water, my whole Being screamed with the pain of the heat against my frozen limbs, a brokenness of Spirit, and an aloneness and hollowness that cannot be described. Sinking my aching and bruised

15

head under water, I sobbed very alone, not wanting to disturb anyone or admit what had just happened.

As the days went by, I told no one. I felt shame. But worse was to come. As the weeks slipped into months, I did not want to face the fact that my period had not come.

Finally, I knew I had to see a doctor, and I chose one that did not know our family. The worst was confirmed. I was pregnant by a rapist whom I hated for what he had taken from me. How could I love this child? The doctor showed no compassion and told me that at sixteen I was old enough to have a child. The fact that it was a rape seemed of no matter to him.

Later, out of desperation, I saw my family doctor, who had been with our family during my father's long illness. He showed more compassion and coaxed me to tell my mother. Abortion had just become legal, but the National Health waiting list was six months long. It was not an option. I was already three and a half months pregnant, and every day I had wished it were not so.

I will always remember the day when I finally told my mother. She had come home from teaching school for lunch that day. I shall never forget the look of sadness, shock and disbelief on her face when I told her. Why had I not told her before? She could have helped that night had she known. She asked me what I wanted to do. She could not give up her work to help look after another child. She was already supporting three of us kids on her small salary.

Dad had died leaving very little in the bank. She said she and Dad had often said how important it was for me to continue my education no matter what. More importantly, Gran and my Aunt were to arrive in a few weeks. They must never see me like this. This was a matter of family pride. Gran would never let us hear the end of it, and we both knew how she could hold resentment.

I did not believe I could love this child, as it would always be a reminder of that dark night. I would probably blame the child for the rest of my life for ruining everything, though I knew it was not the child's fault. I also wondered to myself what kind of child could come out of a rape where the father was so violent and drunk.

In my heart over the months I had fought with myself. I had always loved the image of the Virgin Mary with the Christ Child. I had always imagined a loving family and children of my own. Now, it felt like everything had been stolen from me. I did not believe I could ever be whole again.

I did not want this child of a rape, but it tortured me to think what the options were. I could not bear the idea of giving birth and giving it up for adoption either. It all seemed wrong. No matter what I did, it would be against some deep Spiritual law for which I had no words.

That same evening, after Mom had returned from school again, she admitted it was terribly hard for her, too, that she had a difficult time even focusing at school her mind had raced so fast. This would, after all, be her first grandchild, but too much spoke against it. She wanted me to have a life and not be tied down so young without finishing my education. Neither could we afford another mouth to feed, but in truth, it was the imminent arrival of her mother that made her take action to protect me. Gran had been very strict with my Mom as she had been growing up. Having a child out of wedlock was something she would not approve of. Mom was a loving and caring person and wanted to protect me from what Gran might say and do. I knew this was horrible for her, and I felt awful to have brought such a problem into her life. We agreed that I must go for a private abortion before Gran and my Aunt arrived. It was arranged, and Mom paid for it from her small savings.

My brothers never knew about the abortion until many years later. At the time, they were told I was staying at a friend's house and had come home with the flu and had to be in bed for a few days. There was no counseling for rape or abortion available in England at that time. The doctor at my check-up the next week treated me like a whore and acted as though I was just another of those girls who got into trouble. I felt completely broken.

It took me a month to get over the wretched pain in my womb from the abortion. The anger I felt towards the rapist did not leave me for several years. The haunting reality that I had taken my child's life never left me, but I hid it very deep. I had to hide it in order to move forward. This would remain a secret between Mom and me for many years.

All of this happened before my seventeenth birthday.

In one year I had seen the death of my father, my friend, and my first child. I was changed. I no longer could believe in a God of compassion. The world seemed to me to be a harsh, cruel place.

✦

Years went by, and I sought to bury my pain in different ways, without any real success. I went through art school and became a photographer and illustrator. It was not until I traveled to Mexico and met the family of Mayan healers that some of this misery was finally unraveled. I was twenty-three years old at the time. These wonderful people taught me how to use my gifts of sight and helped heal me from some of my pain. They worked on the wounds of the rape, as well as events from past lives, which they said were affecting my health in this life. They taught me to forgive and about their system of healing. They also re-introduced me to Christ and Mary and the Angelic kingdoms.

Their belief system did not come easily to me, as I had thrown out many of the Church's teachings when I was sixteen. I still doubted a great deal, though I did have a basic belief in some Presence greater than myself. Their healing work eventually brought me peace, and I felt happy to be accepted for who I was and to finally understand my gifts. They told me I was destined to become a healer and that we had known each other in previous lives. The healer had foretold I would come to them two years previously. Her son and I spent many hours together and fell very much in love. I became pregnant again.

I knew the instant I became pregnant. I felt my body change, and I could see the misty Light of the Spirit-child as an undefined hovering orb with me. However, I did not know how to speak to this child, or even that I could. Here I should have found joy, for this child was created with love, but it scared me to be pregnant again. A deep-seated fear arose linked to the memories of the previous pregnancy. A thought form at a subconscious level made me want to run like a terrified fox before the hounds. I wanted to hide the fact from my lover's family. All the old fears about being rejected, especially by my own family, came up again. To be sure I was pregnant, I went to an old healer from another part of town who confirmed the pregnancy before my period was even due by passing her hands across my belly and feeling the child's Spirit there.

Now I faced a similar dilemma as I had when I was sixteen. I could not face going home to my mother's house pregnant again. Gran's rule still existed, and she had been harsh when her own brother had made a young woman "from the other side of the tracks" pregnant. I had seen the bitterness and feuding in the family when he married her, and I had seen the emotional damage done to the daughter of that marriage. Also, I knew Gran could never happily accept the darker Mayan blood into her family.

I was not married. I had no funds to support a child alone. I had no health insurance in Mexico, and my lover was in college and had no funds either. I panicked and decided against his wishes to have a backstreet abortion, borrowing the money from a friend to proceed.

When I had faced this dilemma at sixteen, the pain had so hardened my heart and cut me off from my true feelings that now I felt abortion was still the only acceptable way out. With hindsight, it is strange to see how a pattern can become so aggressively fixed when it comes to survival and acceptance within a family group. I have seen this many times since with other women.

I knew that getting it over with quickly was the best thing to do, and within six weeks of conception I went through the highly illegal procedure in Mexico City. Here in a city of Catholics, I found a thriving backstreet business. It was all cloaked in secrecy, requiring two safe houses to move through, and prepayment of a large sum equivalent to probably two or three months wages for most women in that area, before I even got to see the doctor. The last part of my journey, I was blindfolded, turned around three times, then walked the last few streets to the doctor's office by a nervous woman who said this was to protect all those involved. I was to speak to no one when I got there.

Many women were there in a room, waiting in hushed silence. No one dared to speak, or let the others know who she was. One by one we were led to a small room. The doctor and nurse worked quickly. They sedated me by injection only long enough for the procedure.

I regained consciousness in a recovery room to find myself bound with heavy napkins and cramping. I was blindfolded again and quickly ushered out the back door and led back to the safe house before being released and met by a friend. The whole visit lasted less than an hour. I felt a sense of relief that it was over and tried to put it behind me, but my Mayan lover was greatly distressed by it all, and spoke of karma and sins against God that we would pay for many lifetimes. I did not understand or believe much of what he said at the time, as I had no belief system to comprehend such things.

I prayed I would be forgiven, and I know he also did many prayers, for he was a healer-in-training. He had wanted me to stay and have the child even if I eventually returned to England. He wanted me to leave the child to be brought up by his family, but I could not bear the heartbreak of having a child in Mexico if I was not to be there. At that time we had no plans to marry.

Within the next month he did ask me to marry him, and I agreed. In order to do so I had to return to England to settle my affairs. There I faced great resistance from my family to the marriage. Though my Mom, as always, was as supportive as she could be, Gran spoke against it, and to my great sadness, so did my Godmother and neighbors, who held many racial prejudices. Many things came against the marriage. In the end it did not happen, and it was my fiancée who said I must continue my Spiritual journey in England, not because we did not love each other, but because that was where I must continue to learn my path of healing alone. It was where I belonged.

So, with great sadness, I let go. In truth, I knew it would have been a difficult life, as many of his relations did not accept me either for similar racial reasons.

✦

England and its grey weather was a different world after the sun and color of Mexico. I had been gone almost two years but had known the Mayan family less than four months of that time. What they had taught me took almost ten years to fully comprehend.

I traveled widely in Britain seeking answers and learning other methods of healing. I met other healers, and we became friends and shared experiences. One of the healers was a homeopath who told me my body was screaming for a remedy which he sent me without telling me what it was for. When I took it, something strange began to happen.

That night it was as if my body was going through a complete pregnancy for each of the abortions I had experienced. I was now twenty-eight years old. My belly became swollen, and I seemed to give birth, though not in a physical way, but as if it was happening at at some other level of Being. The first birth revealed a small girl's Soul, and in the second pregnancy and birth a boy's Soul emerged. These two Souls were quite different in their manner and attitude. By this time I had learned to see and understand the Spirit worlds with more clarity, and I knew these would have been my two children.

I cried a lot that night. My body was going through an emotional completion that I had never had. With the first child, I had always felt I took the only course open to me, whereas with the second, who was conceived out of love, I was angry with myself for being such a coward and for not standing my ground and allowing this child, who now stood before me, a chance of a life. He clearly was a highly intelligent Soul, while the little girl seemed to be of a lower energy and more damaged by the experience. She had been created out of rape by a drunken youth and had been tormented all through the pregnancy by my fears, confusion and desire to be rid of her.

The only hope I had now was that neither she nor the boy had felt any physical pain, as they had been sedated along with me when they were taken from my womb. I asked forgiveness from these two children for what I had done. I asked that Christ and Mary heal them with the Light of Love, and forgive me, and that the Angels gently guide the children into the Light.

The boy smiled and was full of energy and shining blue Light as he left. He simply said "Bye, Mom!" as he went into the Light like a blue shooting star, doing a complete loop around me before leaving at high speed. I realize now that my Mayan lover had probably done much of the healing work for this child years before.

It took longer for the little girl. She was shy and nervous and had obviously known much trauma. There was a lot of damage in the area around her head. I felt that had she been born, she might have been retarded because of the difficulties we had faced together and my rejection of her early on. I was very sorry to see her so damaged. A gentle pink Light surrounded her as the healing work began, and as the Angels lifted her slowly, she fell into a deep sleep.

How can anyone explain such a thing to others who have not seen and felt the same experience? Guilt never left me. It was, in fact, all the more pronounced along with the grief, but I was grateful that at least they were now free and in good hands.

When I asked my friend what he had sent, and told him what had happened, he was overjoyed.

> "Great," he said, "I could tell your body needed completion from an abortion. I sent you the strongest potency of the homeopathic remedy Staphysagria. This is a classical remedy for rape, rape anger and the effects of surgical procedures, such as abortions, though not everyone would

have the same experience as you had, since no one else is quite as sensitive!"

✦

Many years had passed since I left Mexico at age twenty-three. I continued my art, photography and research into healing methods. Then, when I was thirty years old, I married a man from California, whom I had met at a Spiritual community in Scotland. This was not an easy marriage. He was a wonderfully talented photographer and landscaper, but he had violent, uncontrolled rages that were sparked by a severe sugar imbalance and a history of a difficult childhood. On some days he could be as sweet and understanding as an Angel, while on other days he behaved more like a raging alcoholic, even though he never drank.

When I became pregnant, my husband was full of rage, as he felt we could not afford a child at that time. My period was two weeks overdue when I told him I was pregnant, and that I could clearly see the child's Spirit beside me connected with a golden cord of Light to my belly. My husband hammered his fists down hard on the table.

> "Then you tell that dammed child to go away; we can't afford it!" he screamed.
>
> I winced and leaned away from his fists as they struck the table again.
>
> I said to the child, "Look at what is happening here, I beg you to choose another path, I cannot ask you to stay in such violence, please think this through for all of our sakes. I see you are a beautiful child, but this is not the time or place. Please take care and reconsider."

With that, the beautiful child looked at me in silence and nodded sweetly, his eyes summing up the situation. A golden Light hovered around him. He had the impression of a seven-year-old with blonde hair. I could not bear the idea of him being hurt, as I knew he would be if he stayed. I had already experienced violence with this man.

My heart went out to the child, and he understood. He withdrew his life force from my womb, and I felt it leave as this happened. He left fading away from my vision as I sensed Angels helping him back into the Light. In half an hour my cervix began to cramp, and my period came down.

✦

I tell this story not as an example of contraception, though I have since heard in India women can also speak to their children in such a way and decide when a birth is appropriate for the family. I tell this story because it is important to understand that the Spirit of a child is lucid at all times. It is possible to communicate with the Spirit, as it is a sensitive Being. As the small body of the fetus is growing, the Spirit of the child is connected.

There have been many arguments among different religious groups as to how connected the Spirit is, or when the Spirit becomes connected to the fetus. I can only say what I have seen and experienced.

My divorce from that marriage after two and a half years was long overdue. My life had been in danger, and I had become very ill. The karma that had bound us was worked out shortly thereafter and I was free to continue my work.

Though I was sad again at losing a child, at least this time the child had been able to make the decision with me, and the transition was easier for both of us. I have never been pregnant since.

✦

In 1998 my Mom lay dying of terminal cancer. The doctors had found a cancer too late to take action, and it had metastasized throughout her body. We had a very open relationship about her process of dying, and she had made it clear it was her time and all she wanted was to be helped into the Light.

> One of her questions to me before she died was, "Did we do the right thing?" I knew what she was referring to. It had weighed heavily on her heart all these years.
>
> "Mom," I said, "we did what we thought was best at the time. It would have changed my life forever to have had the child. I don't think I was ready. There is no blame. Be at peace."
>
> I could tell by her unspoken thoughts that she felt a sadness that I never had any children and that maybe she somehow felt she was to blame.
>
> "The boys had plenty of grandchildren for you, Mom," I said quietly.

She smiled and looked away. She knew of the second abortion, as I had told her some time before. I had never thought to mention the third child, as he had left willingly and without pain.

Mom's passing was something I shall never forget. The doctor had left us alone, knowing it was her time. My sister in law, a nurse, monitored Mom's pulse, while my two brothers and I sang in three-part harmony our favorite psalm we had sung together in church so many years ago as children. Mom loved choirs and had sung in them all her life. As we sang "The Lord's my Shepherd," I heard her say in Spirit, "That's lovely!"

Her breathing stopped shortly thereafter. She died in peace, at home with her family as she had requested.

She reached the Light.

Two years after Mom died, I was visited by a seer who happened to be traveling through my area. Though I had maintained contact with my Mom in Spirit, it took this visitor from another country to speak about something with which my Mom needed help.

"She is asking where are your children?" said the seer. "She has been looking for them but has not found them."

"Oh!" I said, "You mean the children from the two abortions?" I looked up at the seer a bit stunned.

"Yes, she cannot find them. She wants to be with them to help them and teach them, and to show them the love she could not give them in physical life."

I felt a pain in my heart, realizing how much this would be like my Mom to want to nurture her own and spend time with them. I had not even thought to help her find them.

"I asked the Angels to take them into the Light for me," I said, "I don't know where they went, but I shall ask them to help Mom find them."

Immediately, I spoke to the Healing Angels that work with me to guide Mom to the children wherever they were. They confirmed they would do all they could to help her.

✦

The next day alone in meditation and prayer amongst the trees, Mom arrived with the two children hand in hand, smiling and happy. She was radiant, and both children were clearly overjoyed. The children ran to me and hugged me. There was a healing for us all at heart level. A warmth and joy spread through me that I had not felt before. I asked them their names. Mom said she was calling them Sally and Johnny, though they probably had many other names. She laughed and tousled their hair. Sally and Johnny explained that they wanted to help me help other children.

"Of course!" I said, "It makes sense. That would be wonderful!"

"We want to be guides and helpers in the children's work," said Johnny.

Sally nodded and looked hopeful, her eyes shining. She had come a long way since the time the Angels took her into the Light. Her Soul was now bright and clear.

We all hugged, and as we did so, I could see other family members beside me who had passed into the Light in the last few years, smiling.

"We are as one family," I heard someone say and felt Christ's presence beside me.

That day a lot of Light came back to my heart and womb. I felt whole again.

✦

Because of all I have learned, I have been able to help many clients through difficult times around the loss of a child. I also work with losses of other family and friends. The main purpose of this book, however, is to teach those who may never meet me find a way to ease their pain and the pain of those Souls trapped between worlds, Souls that cry alone.

✦

25

The Voice of the Unborn

Since I began my counseling practice, I have witnessed so much from the realms of Spirit in relation to miscarriage, abortion and stillbirth that I feel a need to share it with others. Though each of these situations occurs for seemingly different reasons, the effect on the child's Spirit, as well as on the mother and father, can be equally devastating.

I know for some reading this it will be difficult. Speaking of abortion in the same breath as miscarriage or stillbirth seems an anathema, since one is self-induced and the other two appear, at first sight, to be the will of God.

Let us look further.

I have extreme compassion for all cases and do not judge a woman or man who comes to me with any condition. I simply observe and help as we take care of the child's Spirit and heal the client. The point is, we are all deeply affected, men included, whether they knew of the situation or not. If the relationship ended early in the pregnancy, many men may not consciously know if their spouse or girlfriend has had an abortion or miscarried, or even in some cases, that they have conceived a child who was stillborn. However, in most cases, I will see the damage in the auric field of all concerned.

In a normal pregnancy where the parents come together in order to conceive willingly, a Spirit responds to their desire, and an agreement is made between all three at the level of Spirit. Again, whether the parents are conscious of this or not depends upon their belief system as well as their level of understanding of the physical and Spiritual worlds. But at the highest level agreements are made and sometimes have been made for generations. Hence, in some cultures such as the Tibetan or Native American, the elders will recognize their ancestors as they are reborn, and those children will recognize their own families and even their old toys.

However today, in this Western world, most parents are unconscious of their agreements, though some may have a deep feeling that this Spirit who is born as their child reminds them of some other family member who has passed on. Or perhaps the newborn has a look of a brother or sister or an old friend from somewhere long ago, but the parents have no proof or witness to this inner knowing. There are few accepted elders in communities who can "see" the truth and confirm what parents intuitively know.

✦

When a pregnancy is desired, and all other physical health conditions are met, such as before conception and during pregnancy, the parents eat the correct foods, avoid drugs, coffee, alcohol, drink pure water, love and accept the incoming child willingly, are under no severe stresses at home or at work, have no family inherited conditions, and are not affected by toxins from the environment, then it is likely that the child will be born healthy. There are many factors in the health of a child, but perhaps the strongest factor is the parent's true desire to have a child.

Anger or hate towards an incoming child severely affects its growth patterns. If a mother or father does not want a child for any reason, it will undermine the Spirit's attempt at growing a healthy body. Chemicals in the mother's body created by fear, hate or anger disrupt the balance of the child's cells as they grow. Negative emotions in a mother's body create an acid condition in the blood which promotes the growth of unhealthy cells and allows infections to harbor in her own body and depletes her immune system. This then sets up the conditions for a sickly child at best, or at worst a child that no longer is able or willing to stay in the womb. All levels of the child's development are affected by the parent's attitudes during the gestation time. This should be a holy time for all involved, a time of prayer and thanksgiving and joy, but sadly this is rare in many families.

I have great compassion for women who miscarry or have a stillborn child. It is a tragedy. I do not want to place blame here at all. Over and above the emotional problems a woman may face in being pregnant, her child may die because of many hidden environmental or hereditary conditions. How could anyone know or understand all the conditions that can hurt a child as it grows in the womb in today's stressful and chemically polluted world? Every year more chemicals are used in the environment without proper testing.

Now many women miscarry because of a lack of natural progesterone in their bodies. This hormone helps the child stay in the womb to full term, but petrochemicals in our foods, water and environment have severely altered our hormone balance, causing spontaneous miscarriages. To understand more on this subject please refer to the books and tapes by John R Lee, M.D., listed in the Reference Section.

This book is about the many women and men who have sought counsel from me because of various conditions they have had. It is particularly focused on the effects on the health of my clients following the death of a child who has not had his or her voice heard nor been given the proper rites of transition, whether the child was carried to full term or not. What does this really mean? The grief of a parent is one thing. The grief of a child who has died and not been guided back into the Light is something else again.

I am often asked why God does not simply take care of this. My answer is because the parent has not let go emotionally and is still holding onto this child's Soul so it cannot leave easily.

Why would a woman who sought an abortion still be holding on to the child? Or why would a parent who lost a child to miscarriage or stillbirth not let go?

This works at many levels. In large part, this is so hidden from clients that they are not aware they *are* holding on. Sadness and grief can be like black sticky emotional glue that binds the child who is trying to leave its parents after a difficult death. So let us look deeper.

Healing needs to take place at all levels for all parties concerned. When we say we have let go, we may have stopped thinking about a situation, but there are many levels of the body matrix that still remember. It is to these

29

levels that we must go for complete healing. These levels are discussed in detail in the next chapter "Seeing Beyond the Physical Realms."

✦

In my work I refer to seven basic levels of Being. There are names for each of these levels. Other practitioners may have different names for them. For clarification I will give a brief summary here:

I call the Spirit or aspect of God within us the Higher Self. This is the eternal part of our Being that never dies. Below this is the Soul, which holds many memories from this life and from previous lifetimes as well. Then there are the following: the Mental Body, the Astral Body (or Dream Body), the Emotional Body, the Etheric Body and the Physical Body (which includes the DNA). These seven levels, plus the seven major Chakras, which are spinning vortices of energy at the crown, brow, throat, heart, solar plexus, sacral center and base of spine, keep our Being working. If any of these levels, or any of the Chakras is out of balance it will cause illness. Lastly, there is the Inner Child. I have come to understand the Inner Child as a composite of all levels of a person. It represents the Sacred aspect of our Being and is centered within the heart. It holds the divine matrix, or seed of knowledge, with all the potential for this life. It is the holder of the life mission and purpose. If a person has faced trauma in childhood, or the life purpose is thwarted for any reason, the Inner Child will be split off from the heart and may become angry or listless, causing a disruption in the life force. With the Inner Child split away, a person may no longer have the heart to live, or may no longer know who they really are, and drift like a ship without a rudder throughout life. The condition of the Inner Child is often the key to many illnesses that are otherwise hidden from view. When the Inner Child is healed and is reunited with the Higher Self and the heart, true healing can begin.

✦

Seeing Beyond the Physical Realm

Over many years I have fine-tuned my sight for Spiritual healing work. I am able to see all the vibrational levels of human consciousness. This means seeing beyond the physical plane and encompasses the seven levels of Being, plus the DNA, the Chakras, past lives, other time lines and the Inner Child.

I always call upon many helpers before I begin my healing work. First I call the Archangels, Michael, Gabriel, Uriel and Raphael to protect the four quadrants of the healing space. Then I call in my teams of Healing Angels. Next, I call in the Spiritual Guides and Teachers and Guardian Angels of both my client and myself. After that, I call in Lord Jesus Christ to my left side, Mother Mary to my right and the over-lighting Angel of the place in which I am working who stands above me. Finally, I call in the pure Light of God-the-Creator to over-light the whole proceedings, while at the same time I acknowledge the beautiful presence of the Spirit of Mother Earth, the blessed Being that supports us all.

I set Sacred space around us all in the form of a golden sphere and ask that our hearts, minds, bodies and Spirits be filled with Christ Light, the Light of Love, and that the work is done for the highest good of all in accordance with God's Holy Laws. Next, I ask that the sphere be filled with Christ Light and I see golden Light pouring into the Sacred space. This brings both my client and myself into resonance with the Light of the Creator and this Light illuminates any issues that need to be resolved as I read the levels.

I always ask that this work be done for the highest good of all in accordance with God's Holy Laws. By doing this, I will not accidentally transgress any cosmic law as my Angels will always let me know if I may proceed on an action or not.

31

Angels are always with us but cannot act for us or stop us from making mistakes unless we specifically ask for their help. It is against God's Laws for them to act without our asking for their intercession. Many people have asked why the Angels didn't just fix things for them, and I respond by saying, "Did you ask them to help?"

Unless you are in a severe, near-death situation, they cannot act for you without your request for help. They cannot take important lessons away from you, but they will try to guide you by speaking into your inner ear or by appearing before you.

Without the help of all these great Beings and Teachers of Light, I would not attempt to do this work. It is with their guidance and help that I am able to proceed. If I see something I do not understand, it is my Angels or Christ who will explain to me what the condition is and where it has come from.

Mother Mary is the one to whom I turn for help with the Souls of children. We work as a team. My role is similar to a conductor in an orchestra as I work with the various groups of Angels, Guides and Teachers moving between the levels of consciousness and different timelines. When I do this work, I am not in a trance state and am fully able to converse with my clients by acting as a link between them and the Spiritual worlds. Sometimes the clients are also able to see those worlds and feel the energies moving if they have developed their sight and have that sensitivity. However, this is not necessary for healing to work.

I am ever grateful to the presence and grace of Christ, Mary, the Archangels, Healing Angels, my Guides and Teachers and Guardian Angels, and all the inner plane Teachers of Light, including, of course the Creator, who is the Source of all life, and Mother Earth, for their love and healing grace.

✦

In session I usually begin at the top with the highest frequency body, which is the Spirit's connection to the Source. This body is the Higher Self. Unless I am told that greater damage needs to be repaired elsewhere, the condition of the Higher Self is the most important. If this is damaged as it connects to the Soul, none of the work done at other levels will hold for long. The Higher Self is our power supply, the link to God-the-Creator. If it is broken away from the Soul, we are unable to exist in the Physical Body.

The Higher Self

The Higher Self, or Spirit, is the aspect of God-Consciousness that is our true nature. It is the individualized essence of God's own Being. Normally, this will show up as a bright Light shining like a star or sun connected by a silver or golden cord to the Soul at a point just above the head. This Light may be overshadowed by events in this or other lives causing it not to be able to reach the Soul in full power. If there is a dark split in the Light, I know either that person had a near-death experience in this life, or life was almost taken suddenly as in a suicide attempt, or it was the result of the parent considering aborting them. In a healthy person, this Light is bright and its connection to the Soul is strong. In a weak person, or in someone with many difficulties, the connection may show up as a very tenuous link. In a person who is fully realized (fully conscious of their God connection) the Higher Self is strongly present and over lights their whole Being with a bright radiance. This is what is depicted as the aura of Teachers such as Christ, Buddha, Saints and healers and is golden in color. This is the ideal state and what I work with my clients to achieve. Clearing the pathways for this state to occur requires work at all the other levels of Being.

✦

The Soul

A healthy Soul should have a bright golden energy that is full of vitality. It should extend several feet beyond the Physical Body, and it is egg shaped. At this level many things can show up. Difficulties in this life or in other lives will show as dark shapes hindering the Soul's progress. By bringing Light to these dark areas, I am able to help my clients process what is holding them back. Here also, I may find the effects of religious beliefs that hold them back. Dogmatic belief systems can be a complete block to the natural life force as it enters from the Higher Self. I have seen many who are very damaged by beliefs relating to guilt and shame they took on early in life. These beliefs can lock up a Soul completely and leave a person unable to receive the fullness of life.

Here also at Soul level and all other levels from this point, the effects of the attachments of discarnate Beings can be devastating. These Beings are not usually evil, just sad and needing help to move on. Usually, it will be an older family member who has not had the closures necessary for them to be free. It may also be a child's Soul who was lost in miscarriage, stillbirth, abortion or sudden unresolved death. Sometimes these discarnate Beings have traveled with the incoming Soul from a past life, as their connections were so strong in the previous life's death process. Peace can always be brought to both parties if the work of release is done allowing the energy blocks to be removed. Then the discarnate Entity is healed and taken into the Light by the Angels.

I have also found imprints from devastating illnesses at Soul level that need to be cleared. There may also be work done by inexperienced healers that can leave damage at Soul level. It is so important to be able to see and know what is being done when you work. Just working on theory without the ability to see is something akin to driving a car blindfolded; accidents and damage are likely to occur.

Additionally, recreational drugs, medical prescription drugs, chemotherapy and radiation can leave great damage at this level, clouding the Soul or shriveling it so that it cannot breathe.

It is with Christ and the Angels that I clear the Soul and recharge it, bringing the Light back in. I always rely on their superior wisdom and healing grace. Once the Soul is clear, it allows the Higher-Self connection to flow more easily to it.

✦

The Mental Body

The Mental Body is the next step down in vibrational frequency. All the bodies are nested something like the Russian doll sets, one inside the other, but always they are interpenetrating each other. It takes time to learn to tune the Spiritual vision to these fine vibrations. In a normal condition the bodies are egg-shaped and extend out beyond the Physical Body to varying degrees depending upon the health and vitality of the person. The Mental Body, however, can be very contorted and anything but egg-shaped with all kinds of influences pulling it out of shape.

I have seen many so damaged by negative thoughts, accidents and violent acts by others, that they have become more like spiky black barbed wire than a clear radiant lemon-gold translucent egg. Here again, I will bring Light to the dark areas in order to see what has caused the various anomalies. As Light is brought in I can see images like watching a movie in full color. They may be from this lifetime or another, but the images are

34

full of energy and show me what has happened to cause the damage. Most times, the client easily remembers images from this life as I describe what I see.

Few clients remember past lives in detail; however, some will have an inner knowing about something they know is real, as they are very often attracted to that time period by historical research, antiques, clothing or jewelry. Some clients will have a complete aversion to those same things if the life was tragic or tortured. At this point, I describe in detail the people and surroundings in that past life and the karmic lessons to be learned. We can then do the necessary forgiveness and closures with whomever was involved in whatever situation comes up, and we can then balance all the energies again by working with Christ, Mary and the Angels.

For each area of darkness on the Mental Body the process is repeated until it is clear and bright. Often to speed up the process, rather than go through all the details, I will focus on the most damaging situations first, and then do general closures on the rest with a prayer that covers all eventualities using the Christ Light to clear the residues. If something does not clear easily, I will then go into more detail to find the cause. Most importantly, the client needs to understand the lessons behind the problems, which is why I always ask the Angels which area of damage to focus on first. Usually, there is a very definite path of disclosure that needs to happen. Going back to the very first time some issue came up is most important, for therein lies the key.

There may be many repeating levels of damage in several lifetimes keyed upon the original event many centuries ago, or sometimes many thousands of years ago. Once the primary cause is removed, the other overlying lifetimes are dealt with easily.

✦

The Astral Body

The Astral Body, or Dream Body, is very responsive to our thoughts and feelings. It is also easily damaged by drugs and alcohol. Many people arrive with their Astral Body flat out on the floor. This can be from general anesthesia used in major surgery, or from drugs or alcohol. General anesthesia seems to knock the Astral Body into a very weakened, comatose state. It can remain in this condition for years after the surgery leaving folks constantly dragging and feeling tired. A healthy Astral Body is essential for us to be able to recharge ourselves during sleep. It is with this body that we are able to return home to the Spiritual Realms of Light for education at the highest levels. However, many folks do not know how to control the Astral Body and end up in the lower Astral realms while they sleep. This is where bad dreams come from. Many discarnate Beings who have not reached the Light are stuck at this level and can influence the dreamer. Drugs and alcohol most often will take us to those lower realms. These substances can stop the Astral Body from rising to the Realms of Light and will keep the dreamer stuck in the lower realms "hallucinating." In my view, these are not hallucinations, but are images from the lower Astral levels with a real life of their own and can be very disturbing. Sleeping pills drug the Astral Body into a kind of blind stupor so that it cannot leave; hence, the heavy dreamless sleep of a person using such pills. The Astral Body then never gets into the recharge zone of Light, and so the person is always tired.

The Astral Body can also be thrown way out of alignment during a bad car wreck or other sudden impact. I can always tell from what direction a person was struck by the displacement of the Astral Body in relation to the Physical Body. I have a team of Angels that works specifically with the Astral Body to bring it back into balance and rebuild it if necessary. Many other things can affect the Astral Body. Negativity of any kind will tend to send it out of alignment. Severe pain, for example, will make the Astral Body leap out of the Physical Body and refuse to come back in. During physical violence or emotional abuse the Astral Body will usually attempt to leave. This is why sometimes a person cannot remember in detail what has just happened. The Astral Body is one of our key witnesses. I find that as I communicate with the Astral Body, once we have balanced it up to a place it can speak to me, it can often tell me in great detail what happened in an accident. This is a very sensitive body.

✦

The Emotional Body

The Emotional Body is one more step down in frequency. It is through this body that we feel our environment. We know way more through our Emotional Body than most give credence to. The "feeling" that tells us something is wrong is from our Emotional Body.

The Emotional Body can be very damaged from trauma in this life and others. It should be egg-shaped and clear and bright. It is rarely clear on clients when they arrive for their first session. Often the Emotional Body is lumpy and looks like a heavy overstuffed pillow bulging in all directions. It may also have big black holes. In general, the energy when it is tired at Emotional level is greyed out and sluggish, lacking any vibrant life force. It can also have dirty, black-red colors representing old hurts and rage, or can be dirty green with old envies, or filthy yellow with jealousy. Indeed, all the ways we describe these lower emotions are actual vibrational colors on the Emotional Body. The aim in healing is to forgive and release old negative feelings that no longer serve us. As I bring Light into an area, I can see what has caused these hurts and wounds. This is one body that may often have discarnate Entities attached to it. In all cases, Christ Light is used to heal and lift those Entities who need to go into the Light, while at the same time forgiveness is done between the client and the Entity who was stuck.

If we do not let go of our grief, guilt or other unfinished business when a loved one passes on, we may bind them to us fully or in part. My work helps clients have final closures with those who have passed on. Constantly bringing more and more Light into the Emotional Body allows a purge of old issues until the body is fluid, shining and golden again as God intended.

✦

The Etheric Body

The Etheric Body is the electrical matrix that acupuncturists work on when they place their needles to adjust the flow of Chi, or life force. All the meridians, or energy circuits, operate throughout and around the physical structure. Without the Etheric Body there could be no Physical Body. Manifestation into the physical comes first from the Source, the Creator, and gradually solidifies down through the various levels of manifestation becoming more and more solid until it reaches the physical plane of existence. The Etheric Body is a beautiful golden network of Light. Where life force or Chi flows freely in the Etheric Body, the physical cells which are served by that life energy have vitality. If the meridians or circuits are blocked or broken, cells become sick and begin to die through a lack of energy.

The Etheric Body can be thrown out of alignment or damaged by a heavy fall or blow. Hence, when I scan the Etheric Body, if I find blockages or breaks I will bring Light into that area to determine what has caused the problem. Sometimes I will see, for example, a break in a leg on the Etheric meridians with the Etheric Body still twisted in the way of the original break and not in alignment with the Physical Body. The client will confirm that the leg was indeed broken and is now healed, but perhaps weakness or pain persists.

> One client, when I looked at him in a lecture, had both his Astral Body and Etheric Body out of place and thrown in the same direction. I asked his wife if he was clumsy and stumbled a lot.
>
> "All the time," she answered. I asked how long had he been like it. "Seems like forever," she said.
>
> His guides told me it happened twenty years ago. The man then remembered he had fallen off his motorbike twenty years ago and had been thrown in the same direction that the Astral and Etheric bodies were now lying.
>
> "But that was twenty years ago," he said.
>
> I said that it did not matter how long ago it was, the damage had not been repaired. He came for a session, and we did the repair. Later, his wife told me that he no longer stumbled, and other problems he had, such as back pain, have now disappeared.

In order to do the Etheric Body work, my team of Angels who work on that level begin by gently lifting the Etheric Body out of the Physical Body so I can view all areas more easily. Often, it is here where I will find energy sacs of deceased Souls from stillbirths, miscarriages or abortions still attached to a client. We then do the necessary release work for that child's Soul. This alone can be a major reason for physical pain in a woman's body, as the grief and entanglement with the child's Soul from this event will block her Etheric flow causing the Physical Body to become ill and register pain. It is on the Etheric Body that I may see the effects of a hysterectomy or other surgery that has left holes in the energy field and subsequent weakness in the Physical Body. By reconstructing the Etheric

Body to its original perfection the correct life force can flow again to cells that have begun to die so they can be healed.

On the Etheric healing team I often have doctors who have passed on and are now in training with the Angels on these subtler levels. Some of their comments can be quite strong as they witness the damage that was done by their physical counterparts on Earth! Many surgical operations leave the Etheric Body in a state of chaos. It is here that our physical doctors need to understand the subtler fields of energy work if they wish to see rapid healing in their patients.

One note here: epidurals seem to cause enormous damage at this level and impede the life force as it flows up the spine.

✦

The Physical Body

While my Astral and Etheric teams work, I begin checking the Physical Body structure, scanning cells for a healthy vibrational sequence. The cells should have a bright field around them and a clockwise rotation in the field. Again, this is subtle to see. If the cells' rotational field is going in a counter-clockwise direction, I know they are diseased cells. If the Light is very dim or dark, I know the cells are heading into serious illness such as cancer. At this time I also check the DNA structure to see if anything is out of balance, and if anything is damaged, I request the desired correction from the Creator. I watch to see that it is done.

Often times, if the liver is heavily congested, the cellular energy will read as heavy, slow and dark red. Likewise, any other part of the body that has darkened colors tells me where sickness is. To counter this, I use a series of Light baths which Christ, Mary and the Angels create. Colors of different hues, strengths and vibrations are radiated through the body starting at the top of the head and passing through the whole length of the body.

Many times as this is done, old dark thought forms, and sometimes Entities, are purged from the physical matrix. By watching carefully I can discover what is behind the illness, and we can do the necessary forgiveness and closures. Once they have been healed and forgiveness is done, Entities, are taken into the Light. Negative thought forms are dissolved, and energy belonging to the client is returned as Christ Light.

Energy belonging to others, if they have been involved in the creation of a thought form, is returned to them as purified Christ Light.

A thought form is a thought that has been energized with emotion and can act negatively or positively upon the body, depending upon the initial intent. A negative thought form is filled with negative emotions. Negative thought forms are often created subconsciously when trauma occurs, and if not dealt with quickly, can begin to take over the body without the conscious mind being aware of it. Thought forms can be created by the individual alone, or in concert with others, or by others acting upon the person, as in brainwashing, ritual magic or abuse of any kind. It is always important to check where the energy has come from and correctly return it as Christ Light to its origin. Once the physical cells have come up to a level of brightness for health, we can move on to the next phase.

✦

The Inner Child

When I talk of the Inner Child, I consider it to be the Spiritual aspect of a person that came into incarnation aware of its Spiritual mission. For health to be vibrant, the Higher Self and Inner Child should be in total harmony. The Inner Child is the part of the Spiritual essence that incarnates into the Physical Body and remains connected to its Source and Higher Self through the heart center. When the Inner Child is on track and has no bad events to throw it out of balance, a person is usually right on target with his or her mission and happy doing what they came to do. When a person has been thwarted early in life, the Inner Child's mission gets sidetracked. The Inner Child then becomes sad and distant. Nothing seems to go right, and life is a mystery. The "Why am I here?" never gets answered.

When I look at the Inner Child, if it has gone through trauma, I may see a very young person, sad or angry or hiding and no longer in the heart center. If this is the case, his or her life force will not be flowing well. Sometimes, if the pregnancy was unwanted, the Inner Child will not have even gone beyond the fetal stage. My team of Angels and I work with the Inner Child to find the wounds and release them so that he or she may be happily reintegrated with the Higher Self and the heart energy field instead of being splintered off from the Source.

As with the Astral Body, the Inner Child can often relay information to me about events my client may well have forgotten. Once these issues come to light, and memory is jogged, the situation is usually remembered and can be cleared.

I have seen the Inner Child in various states of anguish, but once relieved of trauma, he or she becomes peaceful. After that, my client also finds peace.

✦

The Chakras

Towards the end of a session we reintegrate the bodies carefully. My Angel teams make sure all parts work seamlessly. The Etheric Body and Astral Body are brought back into the Physical Body, and Inner Child is brought back to the heart center. Then all seven levels are balanced and aligned with the Source. Then I check the Chakras. It is very rare at this point that the Chakras need much work, other than perhaps bringing them up to a more vital level, as the major work has already been done on all other levels.

The seven Chakras are spinning vortices, which allow the life force to enter from the Source. Crown, brow, throat, heart, solar plexus, sacral and root, all must function. All Chakras, except the crown and root also have similar positions on the back of the body that are directly connected to the ones on the front of the body. The hands and feet have minor Chakras, which I also check. Once everything is working and I have checked all levels for integration, we are ready to move to the last part.

✦

Bringing in Higher Self

Bringing Higher Self into the conscious body now becomes easier as all the major blocks are removed. This can be the most gratifying part for me, as I am able to witness the beautiful radiance of this individualized aspect of God coming into full power in the body of my client. Often with it are tears of bliss from my client. Few have felt such joy and grace in this lifetime. It is a very Sacred moment. We bring in as much energy as the newly balanced body can handle. In future sessions we continue the process, clearing any issues that have surfaced since the last session. In each session we refine the seven levels so that they can hold more Light.

I call it coming home to Oneself. It takes time to prepare, but it is worth every step of the way. Only clients who are truly ready to commit to forgiving others and themselves and are prepared to step into their true Sacred Selves will reach this level fully. One cannot prepare for peace when silently declaring war on oneself or others. I cannot force a person into a higher level of consciousness. The choice is always theirs. Forgiveness and love are the keys. Knowing what to forgive really helps and is where the gift of sight comes in.

✦

All of this is done with many helpers on the inner plane, to whom I am eternally grateful. As I end the session I give thanks to all those who have worked with me, making sure that whatever residual energy within the Sacred space that belongs to the client or me is returned to us individually as Christ Light. Also, I check to make certain any energy belonging to others that we may have been working on at long distance is returned to them as Christ Light. I then ask that the client be protected as she goes out into the world, and that her auric field is sealed with Christ Light.

Once this is done, I close all doorways in space and time that may have been opened for the work. Then I close down the Sacred golden sphere in which I have been working with the help of the Angels bringing all my energy back to myself as Christ Light making the sign of the cross in golden Light over my heart, I simply say, "The work is done. Amen, so be it."

✦

PART II.

CASE HISTORIES

✦

As you prepare to read the following true case histories, please read them with an open mind and a loving compassionate heart.

Each person in these stories was faced with extremely difficult decisions. These very private and heart-wrenching decisions deeply affected everyone involved. Sometimes no decision could be made, and that person had to face a sudden loss without any forewarning.

All of these people need our loving support and thanks for sharing their stories. They have done so with the intent to enlighten humanity and help heal the Heart of the World. Please put any judgments aside and understand the lessons given here are given with love.

If you have been through any situation similar to those described in this section, the prayers in the back of this book can help you. Forgiving yourself and others is essential for you, your family and your lost child's Soul to heal. No matter how your child died, healing is available. You did the best you could with what you understood at the time. Now it is time to heal all involved.

✦

The Rage of Mankind

It was fairly early in my healing work when Mark came to me following one of my lectures. He asked if he could have a private session. I had been accustomed to working mostly with women and their issues, but as he was convinced I could help him, I agreed.

I had been traveling across the United States doing lectures and healing work and never knew from one day to the next who might come to me for counseling. This man was to prove to be a huge lesson for me. He had been in Vietnam in the military and had been married more than once as well as in and out of relationships several times. Mark's problem was rage that could not be controlled, to the degree, he admitted, that only recently in an argument with his spouse, he had taken a shotgun and blown out the TV set. She had left him.

To say I was nervous was an understatement, but my Angelic guides said I must continue with him. There were many levels of Mark that were terribly disturbed, and as we worked through each level, it was clear he had been a warrior many lifetimes. Every kind of battle tool lay around him on the inner plane. One of the Souls with him was a deceased comrade from Vietnam who was still in battle fatigues and had not yet gone into the Light. Battle scenes were still playing out around Mark from many centuries. He was trapped by violence in all directions. His Soul was tortured by the past.

✦

As we gradually cleared the debris from each level, I saw six tiny sacs of energy attached and floating low to his hips and back area. Each one was about two feet long, white and cocoon like. I had seen this before with women who had had abortions, miscarriages or stillbirths, but it was the first time I had seen this on a man.

46

I was fascinated, but hesitated to ask, for surely no man would have allowed or requested six of his children to die? I gently asked if any of his wives or girlfriends had had children.

"None," he replied.

"Did any of them ever get pregnant?" I asked, hoping that what I was seeing was not true.

"Yes, several of them," he said, " but none of them wanted a child with me because of my violence. They all had abortions."

"How many?" I asked.

"Five," he stated.

"Five? Then why do I see six?" I asked again.

"Oh, my God, she didn't! I begged her not to, not the last child!" He sobbed, "She was six months pregnant before she left me! She threatened to, but I can't believe she did it!"

"Let's check it and see," I said gently. "Give me her name, and I will track the connection. There is one child here far more developed than the rest."

So he gave me her name, and indeed the child's energy corresponded to the woman he mentioned.

Now began the release work. For each child I asked a healing Light to come in so it could be made conscious from its tangled sleep. I asked Mark to forgive all parties involved and to ask for their forgiveness at long distance in Spirit. We worked one child at a time tracking each woman connected to the child by her name. As usual, Christ, Mary and the Angels helped me with this. Mary will always hold the child for me while the healing work proceeds. She of all great Teachers of the Light knows the love a mother can give. I am so grateful to work with her.

The most important thing is to very gently bring in the gold Christ Light of Love. Those who do not work with Christ directly should request the healing Light of Love from the Creator.

I have found that the later the pregnancy is terminated, the more rage and damage the child will have. If you are doing this healing work alone or helping another, be ready for the rage of the children as they become

47

conscious, and let them have their voice. Let them speak, let them cry, let them vent their rage and give them more and more love until they can see the reality of Christ and Mary and the Angels with them. They have known great pain and they sense a terrible rejection. They had no way to fight back and so are often terrified. I will always report to my client what is happening because this is their time also to access their own hidden feelings and let them come to the surface.

The dark memories will fall away for the child. The truth that they are Spiritual Beings standing in the Light of God will become evident to them. Just allow them the time. Do not force them into the Light before they are ready. At first, this awakening always brings back the last memories of what they knew, and it was painful. Not all will want to speak, so just let them be healed in the Light and Love of God. Some, usually the early term ones of a few weeks gestation, will just sleep in a golden Light and be lifted that way to Heaven to awaken whole in another realm. Often they have suffered less, as their connection to the Physical Body was not so deeply embedded. They were in a kind of dream state. Even here I will, upon occasion, find great upset if agreements were made in this or other lifetimes by parents to birth this child, who came willingly to them, only to be cast out.

Forgiveness is the most important part of the healing process. A parent must ask forgiveness of the child, and of God and of themselves. They must also forgive the child for any situations in any previous lifetimes that may have caused hurt. For this I always use the "Forgiveness Prayer." (The transcript of the "Forgiveness Prayer" can be found in PART IV of this book under "Prayers of Forgiveness and Transition.")

As the forgiveness takes place, I make sure that what truly belongs to the child is returned energetically to him or her from both parents. Likewise, I make sure that the energy of the parents is returned to them energetically from the child. This is most important, for in the creation of a child both parents share in the energy field of that growing child. If grief or anger is there, it will stop the child from getting into the Light. It will also cause an energetic blockage in the parents' fields, causing them illness.

✦

I have been accustomed to seeing a wonderful gold Light come back into one or the other ovary of a woman, depending upon from where the original egg came.

Now, for the first time, I was witnessing the Light returning to Mark's testes, and by the end of the work a great deal of his own energy as healing Light came back to him. As we did the work to release each child and return Light to both Mark and the appropriate woman, the room itself became brighter and brighter. As each child was lifted into the Light by the Angels, it felt as if a lifetime of burdens was being lifted from Mark's shoulders.

✦

The prayers I use for this process are simple ones, and all are described in PART IV of this book.

I normally use the name of Christ in my prayer work; however, I do have some clients who do not come from the Christian tradition, in which case I may use a modified prayer for their comfort level replacing the words "Christ Light" with the "Light of Love." For me, the Light of Love is the same as Christ Light and is the Supreme Love that radiates from the Creator Source.

I believe that Jesus was a Christed person, meaning that He was over-lighted by and fully conscious of this Light from the Creator. I believe that it was through His conscious Oneness with the Creator that Jesus could heal the sick and raise the dead. This Light is available to all of us for healing if we open our hearts to it. Just as other great Teachers can help people from other traditions, Jesus can act as a mediator for those who ask Him in prayer to help them reach a conscious connection to the Creator's Light within. I have worked with many different people from around the world and have great respect for all the Sacred teachings. In my view we are all from the same Source. We are all within and a part of God, the Creator, (whatever you decide to call this Supreme Being). The resonance of the Creator is Love.

You may speak your prayers as you like, but remember, no matter how many holy names you call upon, it is your heart's intention to forgive and release any sadness or binding between you and another that counts more than just words spoken without intent or belief. A bitter heart will have little success no matter who you call upon for help. Whether you ask the Angels, God, Christ or any other deity to help you, if your heart and mind are not of one accord, your prayers will not have much effect. The desire to forgive and be forgiven must be of a true nature. You must also *believe* you can forgive and be forgiven. Sometimes it is very difficult to forgive past hurts, but it must be done with true feeling so that the binds between you and the other can be released, and your healing can be complete. This is why it is often helpful to have someone lead you in this prayer work to encourage the right focus of intent and keep your motive clear.

The "Forgiveness Prayer" is the prayer I use most frequently in my work. It was taught to me by the Angels. I use it as a transformational prayer between parent and child, or between other parties who have passed on. I also use this prayer for people who are having difficulties in their relationships.

It is most important that the parent speak the words of the prayer out loud. Their spoken word is what will begin the healing for all involved. It is their conscious commitment to healing and their verbal command that gives the Angels and the helpers on the inner plane permission to begin the work. Also, if the other parent is not physically available, I ask the parent who is present to do forgiveness with them using the same prayer (as oftentimes there is blame towards the other party) and also on behalf of the child conceived with that other party.

If I sense my client has not yet truly forgiven himself or herself, I have them repeat several times, "I forgive myself," until I see that it is working. Sometimes they will get all choked up and stop saying, "I can't forgive myself!" At this point, I will coax them on by bringing Christ Light to the locked up area of their body until the tears come and the emotional blockage is finally shifted.

> I tell my clients, "Our anger at ourselves is what can kill
> us. Once the child is in the Light of Heaven, let him go.
> Your rage at yourself only stops the healing work."

As a child is taken into the Light, I use the "Transitional Prayer," also taught to me by the Angels. I watch as the child's Soul is lifted by the Angels into the Light of Heaven. Once they pass through the gateways to the other realms, I ask that the child be healed at that first level and then taken on to the Halls of Light and Learning when he or she is ready. I then seal the door with a cross of golden Christ Light, and the work is done. It is important to seal the doorways after this work is done, so the client's Soul remains firmly in the present moment and is not pulled away from the Physical Body.

✦

In the case of Mark and his six children, his tears were the first in many, many years. Since he was a child, he had bottled up his rage for violence done to him by his father. He also had a great rage towards his mother since birth, as he felt she did not want him. We worked through the forgiveness on these issues, too.

Violence begets violence, and it goes from one generation to the next and one lifetime to the next, unless we step in and take the time to heal it. This is why we must have compassion.

✦

A day later, after the long four-hour session, we had done the previous day dealing with his many levels of discomfort, Mark called me to say he was the most peaceful he had ever been in his life. We had not only worked with the six children but centuries of others who had died by his hands in battle. His Vietnam buddy who had died beside him in battle was now happily in the Light also.

The burden was off of Mark. He was free to make a new life.

✦

The Tragic Miscarriage
of an Abused Woman

Mona's story was a particularly sad one. This was her first visit to me. I worked on clearing many levels of abuse she had suffered throughout this life that had left her in physical pain and emotionally drained. So much damage was evident at all levels it was difficult to know where to begin. Once I had brought her Higher Self and her Soul into a better place, I scanned all her other levels. We worked through the Mental Body and stabilized it by removing a very dark and tormented past life.

Working with my team of Angels, I was advised to separate out all of Mona's other bodies, placing each one individually around the room. I often separate out the Inner Child and Astral Body, but today all bodies needed to be separated quickly so that different teams of Angels could work at different levels with me. We moved between the Astral Body, which had been damaged by toxic drugs and the effects of general anesthesia; the Inner Child, which needed a great deal of cleanup and was tangled in a black web of fear; the Emotional Body, which had a huge gaping black hole in the back; the Etheric Body, which showed damage everywhere from blows; and the Physical Body, which was wracked in pain from everything focused down from the other levels.

✦

I began by bringing a powerful cleansing Light through her Physical Body with the help of Christ and the Angels. This cleansing will literally drive out memories at the cell level. As the old black tar-like images began to seep out of her, I could hear a screaming rage from her womb area. I could see a very violent argument that had taken place earlier in this life, and I saw that she was thrown and struck by some tall, aggressive man. The violence had left a huge imprint in her womb.

> A dark form of a fairly well-developed fetus was pushed out between her legs by the Light we were bringing through her. It was a morbid image. As it came away, I could see it had not reached full term. It was too small and had probably died in the womb. The image of afterbirth was coming away with dark red blood spilling everywhere on the inner plane. There was no doubt in my mind that this was a miscarriage.
>
> I asked Mona if she had had a miscarriage or an abortion. She said she had had both. The miscarriage had come first, and this was what I was witnessing. She had been four months pregnant when her alcoholic husband had violently abused her by throwing her to the floor, kicking her, causing her to lose the child.

Her miscarriage had been a very painful experience in itself in a small hospital unit that provided her no pain relief. She ended up feeling angry, helpless, bruised and battered, with her breasts leaking milk for her dead child. Tears fell as she told me the story. She had left her husband and gone to her parents' house after the miscarriage. She divorced her husband shortly thereafter.

✦

We began the necessary prayer work to help the child from the miscarriage into the Light. In order to expedite the work I requested permission on the inner plane to call in the presence of the Spirit of her husband, who was still living. I often work this way in order to understand problems. I always ask permission of the Higher Self of the person involved, and of their Guardian Angels, before calling the Spirit present. All of our Spirits have the capacity to extend consciousness far beyond the Physical Body at any time. The Spirit must always stay connected to the Physical Body in order for the body to survive. I do not always get permission granted to call someone to a healing. It must be with their permission on the inner plane. Sometimes a person needs to be fully present with what they are doing. Often Angels will report back that a person is doing something that needs full attention such as driving a car.

If I do not get permission to bring a person to the circle, I will project my own consciousness out to them if necessary, in order to read information. Again, this is only done with the permission of the person's Higher Self and Guardian Angels. It is rare that a person's Higher Self or Guardian Angels will disagree with the opportunity to heal a situation, but sometimes I am not allowed to proceed for karmic reasons, because important lessons are still to be learned through the situation. In the case of Mona permission was granted.

✦

I could see her ex-husband was a very troubled man with great dark swirls of energy around him as the Angels brought him to our circle.

Mother Mary had picked up the child's darkened lifeless body from the ground and now held the child gently in her arms as the healing work progressed. As the true life force of the child was returned to her from both parents, purified as Christ Light, and the life force of the parents was returned to them as Christ Light, unbinding the child, great changes began to take place. As the golden Christ Light entered the child, I requested that all wounds be healed between the three of them, and that any karma between them be resolved to the degree that was allowed under God's Law. The child became conscious and let us know the great rage she felt.

This is always the hardest for the Souls who had a difficult death. As they become conscious, they believe they are still in the body moments before death. It is always these last moments of emotional and physical pain and grief in the Physical Body that they remember first. It is like waking from a bad dream. Until we can get enough Light into them to let them see the Spiritual world they are now living in, they are stuck between realities, believing they are still a Physical Being who is experiencing the dying process again.

> The child screamed and wept and took some minutes to be consoled until I could get her to understand that she was now safe and in the presence of Christ, Mary and the Angels. Though she could clearly see me in my Physical Body as I spoke to her, she seemed not to relate to the Angels or Christ or Mary, or even see them as others might in her situation, as her mind was too focused on her anger. This is unfortunately how most of us walk

around, so engrossed in the physical world we are blind to
the Spiritual realities around us and do not see the Light.
Anger and emotional upset will quickly cut off our vision
of the Light around us.

Her little body gradually grew to the size of about a four-year-old
as we gently brought in more healing Light, but she remained solid and
stocky, rigid with anger in her spine. She began marching around the room
venting her rage. She had a strong male quality in her stride that made
me think her last life had been as a soldier or that she had served in some
military capacity. She was still very much involved with the difficulties
this and her other lives had brought her and seemed not to have been
happy for many centuries.

She told me she had planned to cover a lot of ground. She showed me
an old gnarled dead tree marked like a totem pole with notches. She sat
down and leaned up against it, hugging her knees. She said that each notch
was a karma she had hoped to work out in this life. One of the biggest
notches represented what was to be done in relation to her father. He had
killed her in a previous life, and she was coming back to work it out. Her
eyes flashed angrily towards him. Now she could not complete what she
had planned.

The child obviously needed further healing and teaching, as she was
still upset. I knew this Soul needed help in understanding how to proceed.
She had gotten off track many lifetimes ago. I doubted that between lives
she had ever experienced the sanctity of the Light and had most likely been
reborn several times in difficult places because of karmic entrapments.
She appeared not to understand the opportunity for going into the Light or
even that it was a place to go that would help her.

I gently suggested that it would be a happier situation for her to forgive
her father now and allow the healing Light to enter her body. Then she
could let the Angels take her into the Light of Heaven so she could be
further healed. She agreed to go with some reluctance, still not knowing
the beauty of what lay ahead of her. However, forgiveness was another
matter.

I guided Mona through the "Forgiveness Prayer" with the child, and
she asked the child to forgive her. Then I asked Mona if she would also
speak the "Forgiveness Prayer" to the child on behalf of the father. At
first she was reluctant to do so, as she felt it would do no good; however,

I encouraged her to help the child by speaking for the father. Things began to soften and energy shifted between all three.

As the Angels prepared the child to go into the Light, she gave a backward look toward her father that told me she was not finished with him yet. I cannot forcibly remove karma nor would I want to. There were too many ancient battles between this child and her father. I requested that the Angels would help her choose the correct path of forgiveness.

Of the child's own accord, as she was leaving with the Angels, she turned and spoke to her mother:

> "I am sorry he hurt you because of me. I am very sorry. It was not your fault."

With that she went into the Light with the Angels. A lot of Light had returned to her mother's womb, and also to her father, though he still had a long way to go before he would know true healing. That would be a choice made of his own volition sometime in the future.

I wondered about the reason for the father's violence. Was it perhaps that he had unconsciously known that this child meant to have her karma finally finished with him and he could not face that, so he brutalized his wife, causing the child's death in this life? As the child had seen so many difficult lives, did she perhaps come in with revenge on her mind? Had the father reacted to this, or was it sheer drunkenness that allowed negative energies to run through him causing the violence?

I asked Mona to forgive her husband, and as we said the "Forgiveness Prayer" together again, even more Light came back to her. An angry black cloud emanating from him that had been attached to her body had been lifted and dissolved into Light as it was returned to him. This angry cloud was his own life force that he had lost in his violent rages towards her. As we returned it transmuted as Christ Light, it came back as a healing to him. Rage and violence deplete one's life source. Once it is dissolved away into Christ Light, the healing life energy can return and therefore health with it.

Mona then explained that after a year of separation, her husband had sobered up. She thought it was safe to return and remarried him, in part because they had two children between them previously from their first marriage.

She explained that it was not long after she remarried this man that he started drinking and was violent with her again. She was pregnant again but this time she made the decision to have an abortion early in the pregnancy rather than stay with him and go through all the pain again of another miscarriage. She then took her two children away with her. She did not remember much about the details of the abortion, only that it was in a clinic somewhere. She said leaving her husband for good was the best decision she ever made in her life.

✦

> I quickly found the child's Etheric sack floating above her belly. The aborted child was full of sadness as we brought her into consciousness. She was crying and did not understand why she had been aborted. It took a while to bring her back together and heal the wounds. The broken bodies of aborted children have suffered greatly.

She was a pretty Soul once we got her cleaned up, but she also had big issues with her father and was furious that she had not been able to complete her work with him. As she became stronger during the healing work, she actually tried to attack her father, lunging at his face on the inner plane with her tiny hands, as she felt he was to blame.

I intervened with a golden Light from my own hands and caught her before she could make any impact. Stabilizing her, I spoke gently to her and helped her see this would not work, though I fully understood her feelings. I gently put her back into the arms of Mary.

The child wept as we brought her into balance. The more Light we brought into her little body, the stronger and quieter she became, until her Soul was once again fully reunited with her Spiritual Essence, standing clear, and leaving the remnants behind of her brief physical existence as it dissolved into Light. Although this child had shown her anger, it was clear to me she had been able to reach the Light more easily than the first child, between lifetimes. She was a more advanced Soul.

As we took her into the Light, and once all the prayer work and forgiveness was done, she let her mother know she did not blame her for the decision. Though it had been her mother's decision, she knew it was based upon the very dangerous situation with her father. She held only him accountable. This child went into the Light with hope. Mona felt a great deal of relief as the goodbyes were done. Tears had fallen as each acknowledged their love for each other.

The father's Soul had received his energy back from the situation, but I knew his path would not be easy as we sent him back to his body with the Angels. Mona at least was free from her burdens and the rest of the healing work continued.

✦

On the Etheric Body it was clear that massive damage had been done around the womb and ovaries. Mona explained that she had had three operations after the abortion. The first one took part of the left ovary away. The next one took the right ovary. The final operation was a complete hysterectomy and took what remained of the left ovary because of continued pain in that area.

The pain had continued, however, and the operations had been for naught. Perhaps now with the release of all this rage and hurt the pain could finally be removed. Certainly much of the darkness had gone. We did extensive work rebuilding the Etheric Body in that area and all the way up the spine and around her head.

Mona had seen so much violence. I explained to her that we would need several sessions to completely heal the various levels. The work we did that day was just emergency work, but already she looked clearer after only three and a half hours of healing.

With the help of my Angelic teams, we slowly brought Mona back together again. It was not easy for her, as she had many other issues still to face that day in our session. The very real physical damage she had endured in her various battles with a more recent boyfriend would require other specialists in spinal chiropractic work, but at least the children's Souls were free and the Light in her abdomen was balanced again and golden.

Sadly for Mona, violence was all she had known in this life since childhood. Her father was an alcoholic, and abuse was what she had been brought up with. Changing this pattern, which had repeated in all her relationships, was going to be a big task for her.

✦

Later that day, as I was writing my notes, the first child who had gone into the Light in this session sent a message via the Angels.

"The child wishes you to know she has chosen the right path."

✦

I knew then that much of the child's pain would be relinquished. Desiring revenge never brings us happiness and always crystallizes pain in our Being.

✦

The Sadness of Stillbirth

We like to believe in the sanctity of the womb. Traditionally it has symbolized a safe and Sacred place out of which the miracle of new life springs. How is it then that some children go almost to full term and then die in the womb or just as they are delivered? It makes no sense. The parents grieve terribly and wonder what they did wrong. Both parents may inevitably question God's will in taking a new life away.

✦

Again, every situation is different. I have heard women talk of stillbirth where the child was terribly deformed, or only partially formed. One can understand the death of the child in these cases because it simply could not survive without the required organs, yet the parents question why. Sometimes drugs such as thalidomide (which was once given to women to stop nausea during pregnancy) may cause such problems. Chemical exposure in the environment, such as mercury, damaged many children in Japan. Exposure to electromagnetic fields from computers has been found to cause spontaneous miscarriages in pregnant computer operators in England. It is now known that even weak electromagnetic fields will alter the normal cell growth in humans and in animals, creating cancer and abnormal growth patterns. Radiation exposure is well known to cause terrible deformities. Petrochemicals are only now being understood for the extreme damage they are doing to the reproductive systems in both men and women. Our water and food is often contaminated with known carcinogens from petrochemical compounds found in fertilizers and pesticides. Blighted potatoes in Ireland and toxins from mold on corn used for tortillas on the Mexican border are now being studied for the tragic defects they appear to cause in fetal growth. All of these things must be taken into account. No matter what country we live in, we should all be filtering our water and as much as possible staying away from toxic areas and eating organic, carefully washed food.

When a child is stillborn, it is natural for the medical profession to take into account all of these factors, along with genetics and the age of the parents. What they often miss, however, is the underlying causal factors between the parents and the incoming child. If a child is not wanted by one or the other parent, the power of that rejection will affect the growth of that child as surely as a toxic chemical. I have to be careful how I explain this, but simply put, if a mother or the father is depressed and fearful, or hateful and angry about being pregnant, it will affect the mother's blood chemistry. The blood chemistry directly affects the child's ability to grow in a healthy manner. Acid thoughts literally create an acid blood, and acid blood is what sets up a pattern for disease and cancer.

As I was about to begin writing this chapter, Annette came to me for healing. Normally, I would do clearing at every level, but because she had limited time and funds, we worked on what I call "emergency work." She had many questions about her two living children, their lives and directions, and about the sale of a property from a divorce settlement from her first marriage. The divorce had been over for many years, but her ex-husband was now being difficult in negotiations. As we worked through the different questions, it became clear to me that something was very wrong with her cervix and her womb.

> When I asked her if she had any known conditions, she said, "No. All my pap smears are normal and I have no problems there . . . do I?"

> "Something is not right there," I said. " There is so much sadness in your cervix and in your womb, it's as if they are weeping. Have you had any miscarriages, abortions or stillbirths?"

Normally, if we had had time, I would have already scanned every level of her being and most likely seen the fetal sacs, but due to the shortness of the session, I had not reached the vibrational level where this usually shows up.

> "Oh, " she said, " I forgot to mention it."

Tears began to well up in her eyes, "I had a stillbirth when I was pregnant for the first time with my first husband. Actually, it was twins. One died, and the other survived only seventeen months."

"That explains the great sadness," I told her. "Did you give birth naturally?"

"No, it was caesarean. They gave me an epidural because the X-ray only showed one twin, the other baby was breach, and they somehow missed it in the X-ray. I was fully awake when they opened me up. The nurse said, "Oh, you've got twins," and then the room went silent. Nobody spoke, and I was saying, "What is it? What's the matter?" They wouldn't tell me.

She began to cry.

"Put this on the bottom of your feet," I said, handing her a small bottle of essential oil.[1] "This is similar to what the Romans used before they went into battle to give them valor. It will help you face what we must do here." When she rubbed the oil into the soles of her feet, a beautiful scent permeated the room.

"Now take this and rub it in your hands and breathe it in deeply. It is for the release of emotional pain and goes right into the deep part of the brain called the Amygdala, which is where we store our emotional memories. It will help you let go of this pain. It will also help you cry, which is good, because tears are healing, and they change the blood chemistry."

"Now I am going to find the child," I said, shifting my energetic gaze to the appropriate level, "Ah, here he is, here is his cocoon floating in front of you. I am saying 'he,' as I feel this is a boy. Am I correct?"

"Yes," she said, "They were both boys."

I reached out towards the white cocoon and began bringing Light into it from my hands, caressing it gently.

---

[1] *See Reference Section for information on essential oils.*

> "I ask that Christ and the Angels help me bring the Christ Light of healing into this small child, that he may be healed and free." I spoke gently.
>
> Slowly a small child's Soul emerged, looking bewildered at the tiny body before him that was still encased in the cocoon.

Often the Soul of a child will appear much older than the Physical Body in which he was growing. This is not confusing to me, as I know a Spiritual Being is eternal and really has no age. The Soul, which is created by the Spirit, is the first step down in frequency towards physical manifestation. It is the first body that the Spirit created long ago. The Soul can be very old indeed. It is through the Soul's journeys throughout many incarnations that the Spirit learns of the power of creation and learns how to become a fully conscious co-creator with God. As the Spirit returns to a new life in the physical world, the Soul matrix is transformed into the pattern for the new child to be. Included in this template is all of the karma to be worked out from previous lives. Created by the Spirit, the Soul matrix pre-exists as a template for that new body. It contains all the lessons it will need, and all the potential to achieve its life goals for this incarnation.

Now, as I watched the scene unfold before me, this small child's Soul looked to be about two years old in stature. I could tell his Physical Body had died several weeks before he was taken from the womb. I asked Annette if this was true. She told me doctors said he had died sometime before she had the caesarean. They had opened her up two months prematurely because there were problems. The child had been long dead.

> "It shouldn't have happened!" said the child pitifully, "It wasn't meant to happen that way!" He was looking at his little body all twisted up. The energy around it was all grey and black. I explained what he was saying to me.
>
> "The umbilical cord was twisted around his neck. He was strangled," Annette said, in tears.
>
> "Then let's get him all cleaned up; he doesn't need to suffer any more," I said gently.

63

Though the Physical and Etheric matrix had been long gone, what remained trapped was a combination of the other levels of this child's Being as far up as the Soul.

I asked Mary to step forward and take the child's Soul and the combined energies of his small body into her arms, so that the healing work could proceed.

Mary gathered him up, and golden healing Light surrounded him.

> "While Christ and Mary work with him, let's take a look at the other child. I suspect he needs help also." I said, "I imagine no rites of transition were given for the stillborn? Did you have a proper service and burial for the child who lived? Did you name them both?"
>
> My client looked blank for a moment. "I don't know what they did with the stillborn child, where they took him or what happened to his body. We named him Peter. The one who lived we called Paul. I don't guess anything was done for Peter as I think about it. They must have taken him somewhere. Everyone was more concerned about keeping Paul alive, since he was so ill. Paul did have a proper service when he eventually died."
>
> "Then let me see if he reached the Light. Sometimes when there is such a strong connection as this, and one has not gone into the Light, the other will be held back as well. The bonds are strong, especially with twins, and where there is great grief, they often cannot release one other."

I asked the Angels to help me see the other boy's Soul. Sure enough he was not far away and had been unable to get into the Light; however, he was more bound by his father than by his brother. The grief of the mother and a powerful negative energy from the father held him back. There was also a strong link with his brother, but it was one of love. Paul looked confused and disheveled like a lost child, which indeed he was. His energy was grey and dark. Clearly he had been through great sadness and felt abandoned not knowing where he should turn. This was very sad to see. He shuffled in place like a child who felt he had no right to exist on Earth. I felt very sorry to see him so terribly alone.

"Did you want to be pregnant? Did your husband want the pregnancy?" I asked gently, suspecting a much bigger problem. "Something is wrong here with the dynamic."

"Yes I wanted the pregnancy, but I was very worried, too. We had to get married because of the pregnancy. I think my husband wanted the pregnancy . . . " Her words trailed off.

"Give me the full name of your husband. I need to track what is going on here. Something is just not right," I said.

She gave me his name, and I requested permission from the Angels to call his Spirit into the circle. As the man's Spirit approached, I could see that a tremendous black and red anger was all twisted up in his belly and still hooked into the tiny bodies of the children. It was clear to me he had not wanted them, and that his anger had caused a tremendous disturbance in their energy fields as they grew.

"There is a big lie here," I said. "This man was not happy about the pregnancy, was he? It feels to me there may have been another woman involved. Did he really want to get married to you? There is tremendous anger towards these two children from him."

She began to cry. "He would never visit me after the birth. He left me alone. He wouldn't even visit his son Paul and had him put away in a children's home far away in Houston. The poor child was very ill with water on the brain, or something. He was frail and tiny, and his dad couldn't bear to see him. He never even saw him once."

"Do you think your husband wanted to be married?"

"I hadn't really thought about it until now. I guess I didn't want to think about it, but you are right, there may have been another woman. He was away a lot. He had just come back from the Navy. It all fits. I guess I just didn't want to admit it at the time."

"Do you see what sadness is here in your body? All this is being played out through your womb and your cervix. Your body is furious because it never got to give birth properly. It was ripped open, and you ultimately lost both children. There is so much anger here tearing at your body. Let us begin the release work for all of you. It is time. These children need to be free, and so do you. When you get home, I suggest you ask a homeopath for the strongest homeopathic Staphysagria remedy you can get. It helped me go through the anger of rape and abortion. I'm sure it will help you release your anger and emotional pain in the womb and cervix."

So Christ, Mary and the Angels began a healing for Paul, the boy who had survived the seventeen months. Meanwhile Peter's Soul was already looking stronger and brighter. The fetal cocoon and twisted-up memory of his tiny body were dissolving into Light. The main thing was for us to do the "Forgiveness Prayer" for each party involved. First Annette did forgiveness with her two children and we made sure they got their rightful energy back as Christ Light. Then we worked with Annette and her ex-husband and the links between him and the children and herself. As the Light came back to each, their energy fields became stronger. Annette wept throughout, releasing her pain in waves of emotion. The two boys grew in brightness and strength to the size of about seven or eight-year-olds, and golden Light shone around them. All darkness was gone. As I see Souls grow in size this way, I know it is related to the strength they now have and actually has nothing at all to do with chronological age. They ran to each other and hugged as two loving brothers so happy to be free. They were now ready to leave and pointed to the tunnel of Light opening up above them.

"They are ready now," I said with a smile. "They are hugging each other and so happy to be together again. Is there anything you want to say to them before we take them into the Light where they can be further healed?"

"I love you both," she sobbed. "I love you. Forgive me."

"Then in the name of Lord Jesus Christ I ask that these two young boys be taken back into the Light with the help of the Angels so they may be further healed, and as they leave, we give thanks that this is done and close these doorways in space and time. Amen. So be it,"

I said, making the sign of the cross as they left to close the doorway in time.

"Let's be sure now that all your energy is fully integrated back where it should be. For some reason it is not all coming back into your Being. It is bright and golden, but it is hovering around you and not entering as it should. We must have missed something. Let's go back in time to the operating table. I suspect you have a lot of anger with the doctors, plus their own fears are probably all linked into your system too."

"We are going back with Angels now and placing Angels by you and around all the doctors and nurses who were there at the moment you were opened up. Now, let's do our forgiveness with all of them in order to get your energy back from them and to return their energy back from you to them."

We went through the forgiveness work one more time while I watched the whole process, making sure that her energy was retrieved completely as Christ Light and that all the energy belonging to the doctors and nurses went back to them equally blessed.

Immediately it was done; the Light that had been building around her body was now able to enter fully into her womb and cervix. I brought her back to the present time and closed the doorways on the operating room in space and time.

"You should now feel a lot of warmth in your womb and cervix, a healing golden Light which is your own life force coming back to you transmuted as Christ Light, released back from your family and the operating staff," I said.

"Yes, I feel the warmth and the long-standing pain I have had in my back has vanished!" she said with a big smile, "Thank you so much!"

"Your husband has also felt the shift at Spirit level. You may find he is easier to work with on the divorce issues, though at a conscious level he may not understand what has happened. No Spirit wants to walk in darkness with guilt. All this time he was trying to get his energy back but didn't know how. That is why he has been difficult about the property you are trying to sell as part of the divorce. Anger sticks like glue. He had lost a lot of his life force trying to be rid of those twins. In wishing them dead, whether it was a conscious act or not, a part of him died also."

With that, her husband's Spirit spoke:"God, I am not worthy to receive this Light back. I have sinned terribly. Tell her I am so sorry. I am so sorry."

"He is changed," I said, and I repeated what he had just said. "I ask now that the Angels gently lead him back to his body and help him integrate this Light, which is his own life force, back into his body fully. As he leaves, I ask that this doorway in space and time be closed. Amen."

As he left, I could see he had plenty of other issues to work through, but my work was done. I made the sign of the cross on the doorway as it closed behind him.

"I feel so much lighter," said Annette, in tears again, but now joyful.

"A big burden has been lifted." I said, "Now your womb and cervix are full of Light again. That is what I wanted to see."

✦

In this case the Light, which was her own life force now blessed and whole, had come back to her womb and cervix, where most of the injury had occurred. In other cases it may come back more strongly to the ovaries. The pain in her back that disappeared was most likely due to her grief that had been attached to Paul. It had shown up as a dark cord linking them both. Now that it was gone, the pain was gone. They were free.

✦

With that, I did the closing of the Sacred space thanking Christ and Mary and the Angels and all Teachers and Guides in the Light for their work.

> "Congratulations!" I said, "Welcome home, you made it back."

We hugged each other warmly. She was all smiles.

I then asked that she be protected in the Light by the Angels and gave her one last essence to breathe in and place around her energy field.

> "It's beautiful!" she said.

> "It is for protection and helps strengthen the auric field. I use it at the end of each session," I smiled, "it's a special blend of essential oils.[2] I think of it as the essence of the Angels."

✦

---

[2]*See Reference Section for information on essential oils.*

A New Child Brings Healing after a Stillbirth.

I awoke one night from a disturbing dream of my friend Barbara screaming,

"Take it away! Take it away from me!"

I sat up in bed in California and reached for the clock. It was 3 a.m. on a December morning, not long before Christmas. I stared into the darkness towards the Philippines where I knew Barbara was pregnant, almost full term, with her first child. I knew it was too soon for her to be in labor. I had no idea what hour it was where she was living, but I was seeing her in a panic on a hospital bed in pain and tears struggling to give birth, but there was no real help. Where were the nurses? The child was dead inside her and she knew it. She labored long and hard in terrible pain for naught. A great darkness was around her of turmoil, anguish and rage at the lack of help being administered.

I leaned back, feeling great sympathy, but not knowing how to help her. This was some years before I began my formal healing work; even so, I knew that the child could not be saved. I wanted to believe that what I was seeing was not true; however, I knew everything was exactly as I was seeing it. I quietly prayed that God would help her.

About one month later Barbara arrived back in California and told me her child had died three weeks prematurely. When she saw the body of her child she was horrified at its deformities and the dark hair that covered his whole body. She shuddered as she told her story.

70

"It was horrible!!" She said, "No one really came to help me. They gave me no painkillers. They knew the child was dead inside me, and they left me to birth it alone for over twenty-four hours. The nurses only occasionally came by to see me but gave me no help."

She had felt the child's Spirit leave hours before it could be born, but on seeing the child's body she was grateful now that it had chosen to leave.

✦

Today she was feeling bereft, needing and wanting a child so badly. Her body ached for completion. Her breasts were full for the child that had died. She was newly wed the previous year after having waited for the longest time to find a man she could trust.

Barbara said she wondered what could have happened to bring on such a disaster. Had she brought it on herself by climbing a Sacred mountain in the Philippines where black magic was known to be practiced? Had she done something wrong by praying at the mountain shrine for a child? What kind of mountain Spirit had heard her and caused such a terrible fate? Her mind had been awash with fearful images. Was it karma? What had she done to deserve it?

She told me she had prayed every day since losing the child in an attempt to find answers and had decided that it was a Spiritual purging of her Soul. She had been in a very difficult relationship with another man before meeting her current husband. That man had run around on her. She had been furious about it, and it had caused her a lot of emotional pain. Perhaps all that anger had lodged in her ovaries. The entire ten years they had been together, he had not wanted a child. She had been feeling her biological clock running out and she had a pent up anger brewing each year at his non-compliance with her desires. He kept telling her he was not ready, all the while entangling her financially. The night of her loss she had screamed and wept out all of the rage from herself about all of the things that were wrong in her life. Now, she said, perhaps at last she was clear enough to begin again.

✦

As she had been speaking, I could not find answers to all the thoughts and questions that had tumbled from her mind. I was not sure why things had happened the way they had, but I remembered how unhappy she'd been for years until this recent marriage. I was sorry she had been through so much agonizing pain, but she seemed to have come to her own resolve about it all, and it had brought her peace. For this I was glad.

We had spent many an hour in the years we had known each other discussing Spiritual principles, so I knew she understood exactly how thoughts and feelings could disrupt the life flow. Perhaps it was true that her anger had affected the way the child had been formed. She had become pregnant almost immediately after she was married, which was only a few months after her difficulties with her former mate. My focus drifted away from her sad face to a movement of Light in the Spirit world around her body.

As if in answer to her unspoken question about having another child, I saw a very happy little boy in Spirit, bouncing on her knee. He looked strong and healthy, with black tufty hair that stood up on his head in a most comical fashion.

> I leaned over to her with a big smile and said, "Barbara, it is going to be OK. I see you have a wonderful little boy coming to you soon, with black tufty hair that sticks up on top of his head. It sticks up like this . . . "

> With that I stuck my hand up behind my head with my fingers pointing upwards splayed out and wiggled my fingers at her and at him. He giggled.

> "He is strong and healthy with a perfect body, and he is already here with you now in Spirit. Don't give up. Try again soon."

> "You really see that?" Barbara asked, the sadness fading from her face.

> "Yes," I said. "This is a real thing. He is clearly ready to come in and wants you to be his Mom."

> She said, "I have been praying every day for God to help me have another child."

> "Your prayers have been answered at Spirit level. It is going to be OK."

Within the month she was pregnant again. This time all went well and she gave birth to the little boy I had seen. He was, as I had described, born with that tufty hair ready to go!

> Barbara laughed on the phone as she told me about it.
> "Yes, his hair sticks up just like you said it would. We are
> so happy."

✦

Deep-Seated Fears of Sudden Death Triggered by Son's Stillbirth

James, in his early 50's, came to his session wanting to understand his deep fear of premature sudden death. We had worked together before on other issues and had cleared many levels of his Being, but today this was an overwhelming fear that had been coming to him recently for no reason he could fathom. He is a retired military pilot now flying with a well-known airline. He had not been flying the day that the 9-11 disaster struck in the USA, but many pilots like him have been under stress since that time with all the new rules and changes and possibilities of another attack. We followed this through as a possible link, but the lead did not pan out.

I looked back at my notes. Though James had been a breach birth, with a struggle coming in, that seemed not to be the direct link to this problem either.

I remembered that towards the end of our last session, while I had been doing a deep energetic purge through James's Physical Body at cell level to remove a toxic load, I had found a hot, red and black, shiny, thick, vinyl-like substance in his liver and spine. This had the energy and feel of sadness and loss connected to a child that had died in a pregnancy. When I asked James if he had ever lost a child, he replied that his first wife, Pam, had miscarried three or four times, and then they had a stillborn son at thirty-two weeks into the pregnancy. We did the necessary clearing and forgiveness with the stillborn child, who was actually still strongly attached to his mother energetically. I worked long distance with Pam at Higher Self level in order to do this. We released the child with prayer work, and the Angels took the child's Soul into the Light. The miscarriages prior to the stillbirth appeared to have been the same Soul trying to come in each time.

The child's Soul had been stuck for over twenty years in Pam's energy field, but the memory and pain of the event had also stuck in James's field. In clearing the sadness and energetic links to the child, James's liver and spine had become brighter. We had then continued on with more pressing work to be done in that session.

In this current session as I was clearing James's Mental and Emotional bodies, it became clear that a lot more needed to be done on this issue. Rescuing the child had only been a small part of the picture. The stillbirth had had a much bigger effect on James than had previously been found.

James was currently studying to be a Naturopath while continuing a heavy flying schedule. He carried his books with him and studied every night in the hotel on layovers. He had decided to use his first wife Pam's health condition to answer a test question on the use of certain remedies. This had taken him squarely back to the time of the stillbirth event and all the pain it involved.

James is a stoic man. I knew enough of his background to know that tears were not something that had been allowed as he grew up. The Air Force training had been particularly brutal and designed to eliminate those who couldn't take it. I had found enough damage in his system from that training in previous sessions to know that pain was something these men were supposed to be able to take. As I asked him to go back through what happened, I gave him a special blend of essential oils[1] to use. I suggested he place a few drops in his hands and rub it on his chest around the heart and on the area around the liver to help move the constricted energy. Then I instructed him to breathe in the beautiful aroma, as I knew it would help him release the painful memories stored in the amygdala – the memory center in the brain that holds on to pain.

With that, tears that had been long suppressed from the time of the miscarriages and stillbirth began to flow.

James recounted the full story to me. He had been stationed at a military air base when it happened. After a string of miscarriages, Pam had finally carried a baby until almost full term. They had been delighted to think she was carrying the child without any apparent problems. Then suddenly she became very thirsty and wanted to drink a lot. At thirty-two weeks her

---

[1] *See Reference Section about essential oils.*

75

waters broke, and she was rushed to a nearby clinic. X-rays showed that the child was in a breach position with his legs straight up towards his head. The child's heart rate was rapid and weak. James's superior officer, Colonel Tom Jenkins, and his wife Sylvia had accompanied James and Pam to the clinic. James, Tom and Sylvia sat chatting in the waiting area, as those were the days when fathers were not allowed into the delivery room. They were fully expecting a normal birth.

When the doctor announced the child was stillborn, James said it felt like he had hit a brick wall. It was such a shock. There had been no warning that things were going wrong in the delivery room. His friends did not know what to say. Things had taken a drastic turn from the light conversation only moments before.

> As James told me, "An officer does not weep in front of
> his Colonel. I held it in."

James was led into the recovery room to find his exhausted wife in such shock she was totally unable to grieve. She was numb from the whole experience and could not respond to James's hug or look at him. She did not want to hold her dead son. James was given no option to hold him in order to say goodbye. James had no one to hold onto in his grief. His wife was gone from him from that moment on. A wall had come down around her that James was never able to penetrate.

This was in effect the beginning of the end of their marriage, even though they did eventually have a healthy son some time later after much infertility testing. However, Pam never came back from that moment of loss. She could never move beyond it and blamed herself. Their marriage eventually broke down because of her continued long depression. James could no longer handle it. No matter what he did, he could not bring her out of it, and they eventually were divorced. That was many years ago.

They had named the stillborn baby Luke and though he was given a burial service, it was now clear to me from James's story that Pam had never let Luke go, hence the continuing depression. Both mother and child had become enmeshed energetically.

Baby Luke had one leg that was totally straight, without a knee joint. He was also a hydrocephalic, meaning that his head was over-enlarged with water on the brain.

James had pushed all the feelings of this multiple series of losses deep into his system, which is why I had found them locked so deeply in the liver and spine in our previous session. The liver is a classic area for the toxins and thought forms of unexpressed grief and anger to be stored. The spine, when locked rigid with unexpressed grief, is also a classic area for toxic thought forms to lodge.

Now that the issues had surfaced to the Mental and Emotional bodies, we could finish what was needed. There were three groups of energies that needed to be cleared from the event, as everyone who was at the hospital with James had an emotional response whether or not they had spoken about it openly. Each person in the situation was reacting and contributing to the emotional field, and a group thought form was created. All were suffering in their own ways: the doctors, nurses, James, his wife, the Soul of the child, and the Colonel and his wife still waiting in the waiting room. It was not a good time for any of them.

✦

We used the "Forgiveness Prayer" with each of the groups, so that we could disentangle each person's energy from the other.

First, we cleared what was between James and the Colonel and his wife.

Second, we cleared what was between James, Pam and baby Luke.

Finally, we cleared what was between all of the doctors and nurses involved and James, Pam and Luke.

All this clearing was done in the timeline it had occurred by taking the Angels, Christ and Mary back with us to that moment to work with each person.

For each person involved I made sure that the energy that belonged to him or her was returned blessed and purified in Christ Light. This is so important. It does no good to bring back a person's energy from a situation and not to resolve the frequency of grief or sadness. If this is not done, the grief or sadness will continue to resonate in that person's field in a negative way.

Once all the closures were done, I took the Souls of James, Pam and Luke into the Light to the first level together for a moment for healing. I often do this when there has been great trauma in order to clear the entire field back in the time when it occurred. As soon as the Angels let me know all was done, I brought James back to his body in this moment in time. Pam was guided back to her body, and Luke went on further into the

Light to rest. With that, I requested for all sadness and negative energies remaining in the clinic setting now be purged with Christ Light. Then I closed down that doorway in time.

James, after all the release of entangled energies and tears, was finally in a state of deep calm. The Light had come back to him. The fear of his own sudden premature death had been linked to the shock of his son's stillbirth.

At this point, I asked my guides what lay behind Luke's condition. I was given the symbol for biohazard. I asked James if he had been exposed to anything toxic in the military. He said tear gas was a possibility, but I did not get a yes on that from my guides.

Then he said there had never been a time in the pregnancy that Pam did not have some kind of diet soda in her hands. She drank at least two a day. He felt it had a lot to do with the problem. Aspartame is a well-known neurotoxin and known to damage the fetus. I agreed that could have had a lot to do with it. But in the back of my mind there was something else. I would have been shown the symbol for poison if aspartame were the full key to this event.

✦

One day after James's session I received information on the toxic effects of certain vaccines and how damaging they can be for infants who are given them and for the developing fetus. It got me thinking. That would be the biohazard. I phoned James and asked him if he had been given inoculations in the military.

"Yes." James said, "I had many. Because I was a pilot I had to be 'world-wide capable,' which meant many inoculations on a regular basis."

"Did you have a serious reaction to any of them?" I asked.

James thought about it and said, "Yes, one in particular, now I think about it. It laid me out for days with pain and fever. It was DPT."

On checking with his shot record, James found that the DPT shot came sometime prior to Luke's conception.

"I think that may be a key to what happened to Luke," I said. "Though the aspartame could have played a big role, I would not have been given the biohazard symbol, I would have been shown a symbol for poison. I think that the DPT, or another vaccine, or some other biological agent from your military days is the biohazard I am looking for."

✦

We may never know for sure what the causes were for the deformities and death of baby Luke, but James's fear has been reconciled. Luke's Soul is now free.

✦

Why Could my Child
Not Reach the Light?

A woman named Marion came to see me wanting me to clear her energy so that she could reach her Spiritual goals. Already on a Spiritual path, she was Catholic by upbringing and had married young. She'd had an abortion against her wishes early in the marriage, as her husband did not want children straight away. She felt that the Soul of the child should have been able to reach the Light and be able to come in again as one of her children at a later time.

As I did the clearing work, I found the child's Soul trapped in Marion's Emotional body. When I gently began the healing work for the child's Soul with the help of Mary, Marion became defensive and angry. None of this fit with her belief system at all.

She wanted to believe that the child had gone straight into the Light. That was what was supposed to happen at death, she vented. Why hadn't God taken care of this? Why was this mess left behind? Couldn't God figure a better system than this? Why shouldn't a child be able to go straight back to Heaven? The child had done nothing wrong! This wasn't a fair system!

Surely something was wrong with the way *I* was seeing it!

The universe she believed in was supposed to be a clean logical system and not leave disorganized bits of unfinished business.

Clearly the idea that the child had suffered was too much for her to handle. This was not supposed to have happened in her well-ordered universe. Her guilt unleashed a hidden rage and feelings of powerlessness and sadness all at once.

I explained that when sadness or anger or any negative emotion is involved between people, our Souls can become entangled. Those bindings can hold us back at death and make it difficult for a Soul to leave unless forgiveness is done between the parties. Abortion usually causes great upset for all involved.

> Still in a defensive mood, she asked, "Why didn't my guides tell me not to proceed with the abortion if the child would not reach the Light?"
>
> Her guides then quietly spoke to me and asked her two questions:
>
> "How did you feel when you knew you were pregnant?"
>
> "Elated," she said.
>
> "How did you feel at the idea of abortion?"
>
> "Great sadness," she said.

Then they said that they had tried to get through to her through her feelings but she had not followed her heart. She answered that she felt that she had had no choice in the matter because of her husband's wishes. They were young and he wanted time to plan the family.

I said I understood her position and his. This was not about who was right or wrong, it was about healing the situation. Then I began to lead her through the "Forgiveness Prayer," so that we could release the child's Soul and get him healed and into the Light. She was still brewing over the situation, however, not wanting to accept full responsibility for her part.

Then she became upset with the child.

> "Why did the child not know ahead of time that the timing was not right? Why could he not call his Soul back to the Light? Surely the child could see our situation? Surely he knew?"
>
> By now the healing work had stabilized the child enough that he could speak to me, though he was not completely free due to her upset.
>
> He simply answered that he was trapped and could not go because he was cut off from his Higher Self by the act of the abortion and by her emotions, which kept him entangled.

✦

81

Much like others who are suddenly cut short in life through murder, suicide or other violent death, the Higher Self connection was severed abruptly from the body. His ability to easily leave this plane of existence was curtailed. He was given no rites of transition at the time and no help. Until now he had been trapped between worlds.

This was not because she was a bad person or that the child was unworthy in any way. Her sadness and anger at the event, plus unresolved issues with her husband about it, held the child's Soul back. She was not aware enough to give the child transitional rites. Nor did she understand how to proceed. She had never tried to speak with the child at any time and had assumed God would do her work for her.

As far as timing was concerned, I explained that what sometimes seems like bad timing to us is actually perfect timing for the Soul's mission on Earth that he has planned with us. We have often forgotten our agreements while dealing with this earthly existence, yet we are the vessels through which this new Spiritual life comes.

Some Spiritually-evolved Souls have traveled many lifetimes together acting as parents or children or spouses to each other many times over. These agreements are made before birth with parents on the inner plane and the timing of conception and birth have great impact on the universal influences a Spirit may need.

Marion's connection to the child was an old one, and an old agreement had been in place. He had thought she would welcome him, which actually she had at the beginning, as she had been happy to be pregnant. Had her husband understood the full implications of his choice, he may have chosen differently. Abortion can often be considered an easy option when a person cannot see the long-term consequences for all involved.

✦

I explained to Marion that in a normal death process the Soul is on a path of return to the Light. Death is a gradual process of releasing from all levels of the body and a gentle lifting back into the Light via the Higher Self connection to the Source. If the Higher Self connection is abruptly severed, and if difficult emotions are connected to the moment of death which entangle it, the Soul can become entrapped in the lower realms of consciousness and be unable to return to the Light unless help is given.

Likewise, people who have been involved with great darkness and negative actions with others in the world will be held down in the lower levels of consciousness, and they will not easily reach the Light without help.

I continued leading her through the "Forgiveness Prayer."

I asked her to forgive herself, her husband and the child. Then I asked that the child forgive them. This was so all the energies involved could be brought back into balance between them. As this was done, golden Light came back into her left ovary. Light returned to the child and to the father. The tangle of Marion's emotion around the child was transmuted and brought back to her as clear golden Light.

> As we proceeded and the child was healed, I could see he was a very evolved Being. He bore her no anger and just looked at her with the look I have seen in Christ's own eyes at times, a look of compassion and sad understanding of our human failings. He simply asked her, "Why?" He looked more like a father looking at a child than a child looking at his mother.
>
> She looked down. "I am so sorry, I did not know," she said.

Marion felt great remorse. She had to face and forgive herself.

Her biggest grief was that her child had been stopped in his Spiritual journey, because of her action. The freedom of the Spirit to grow was something she held dear in her teachings. She had learned a valuable lesson about Spiritual freedom and taking responsibility for one's own feelings and actions.

The child had obviously come to her because of her Spiritual path and only asked her now to teach others this Truth. Throughout the work he had taken on more and more Light and had now grown to the full stature of who he truly was on the inner plane. He stood tall and strong, a very old Soul, a great Teacher robed in golden Light. After bidding her farewell for now, he walked easily with his Angels into the Light. He needed no guidance as to the way of return. He was home. I closed the doorways in space and time behind them with a cross of gold Christ Light and gave thanks that it was done.

✦

I wondered afterwards, how it was that such a Teacher should become trapped. My Guides told me it happens all too often these days. There is always a risk that a parent may decide not to continue a pregnancy through a lack of understanding and a forgetting of agreements previously made, even when that person is on a Spiritual path.

✦

Her Lost Brother's Spirit Wanted to be Her Son

Jen had seen a very sad life. When she was in her early twenties, her brother had died in a plane wreck. He was only twenty. She had never let him go at an emotional level. The ensuing sadness led to alcohol, drugs and suicide attempts. By the time she was referred to me, she had attempted suicide three times after being given progressively larger doses of Prozac for her depression.

Jen flew in from New York to see me in Texas. She was pale and thin with scars on her wrists. She had no smile, just a bleak worn-out expression. Her body was frail and seemed too fragile for a woman in her early thirties. Her energy seemed scattered to the winds. She was in a bad way. I asked her if she had any belief system at all, and she said she no longer believed in anything. She spoke in a detached, yet hard way, as though she were looking down on a huge black hole that had swallowed her life, and God had not saved her brother or her to date. Nothing made sense to her anymore, yet she was open to seeing what I could do for her based upon what a friend had told her of her own experience in a healing session with me.

> As I worked with Jen, it was clear that her brother John had never been able to reach the Light due to the emotional ties between them. These ties looked like a mass of black thick cords tightly binding them together.
>
> Jen's Higher Self was badly fractured because of her suicide attempts. Her Soul was dark and exhausted

85

from the years of medications and pain. The first thing I had to do was release her brother's Soul into the Light. I explained that she must let him go. She cried saying she feared she might never see him again.

I asked her, "Can you see him now?"

She admitted she could not. She had bound him so tightly she could see nothing and hear nothing from him. Each time he had struggled to be free and return to the Light, she had been pulled towards suicide as the only way to stay with him.

I explained to her that the only way she could heal and that he could be happy was for her to let the Angels take him into the Light. Once he was healed, he could always come back to her, but as it was he could not rest as she was holding him back. They were both exhausted. Once she realized that she was causing him difficulties by holding him back from returning to the Light, she agreed to let him go. She had not realized he was suffering because of her sadness.

With that we spoke the "Forgiveness Prayer" together, and the dark cords began to fall away, freeing them both.

Working with Christ and the Angels, we transmuted the energy of the dark cords into Christ Light and returned to each of them what was truly their own. Jen had expended a great deal of life force to keep her brother's Soul beside her. As the energy came back to her, her auric field began to take on more Light.

As we did the work, her brother John was now beginning to heal. To my surprise as he emerged out of the darkness from which he had been held, I saw him dressed as a young Jewish boy ready for synagogue. This perplexed me as Jen had so strongly stated she believed in nothing. When I asked her why John would be dressed in such a manner she explained that her father was Jewish, her mother Catholic, and that she and John had been introduced to both faiths. It was when John died she had given up on religion. Once we got John all clear, he was smiling, and promised that he would come back to her soon as her guide. They also talked about the possibility of him being her child in the future. This brought her a lot of happiness. Once we had taken John into the Light, we continued on the many other levels that needed healing.

+

The next day Jen called me all excited. She had been having a vivid dream of John, and when she awoke she could see him smiling at her from the bedside. I let her know that usually the Soul needs a rest in Heaven before spending much time as a guide, so not to be surprised if he would be away a while. This was his way of letting her know he would keep his word. In the next few sessions Jen blossomed and became a different person. No longer dark and withdrawn, she was happy and looking forward to life.

Jen and I stayed in touch and became good friends. John soon became her guide and constant companion. They talked often with him teaching her what he was learning on the inner plane. Several times I spoke with him when Jen would come to visit. I could see that he was excited with all he was studying of the ancient Scriptures in the Jewish tradition and that he wanted to teach her so much. He is clearly a high-level Spiritual Being.

+

About seven years had passed since our first sessions when Jen telephoned me. I was in England doing the legal work on my late mother's estate. Jen was in Texas. She was so happy. She had finally found a man she could love and hoped they would marry soon. What a different picture from the first time I had met her. The Light about her shone a beautiful gold. This I could see even from England. Clearly she was in love and in a good place.

> As we chatted, I noticed a soft golden Light hovering next to her belly attached to her. I asked her if she knew she was pregnant.
>
> "Well, no." She said, "Am I?"
>
> "Sure looks that way to me," I replied.
>
> She remembered feeling elated one morning after making love and felt a rush of energy into her womb that made her feel incredibly happy.

"That was it," I said and suggested she get a pregnancy test.

We both knew who the child would be. I told her that all her guides and Angels seemed very happy and excited about the situation.

✦

A few days later she phoned to say that indeed she was pregnant but now her joy had crashed to despair. Her lover was angry, did not want the child, and blamed her for the pregnancy. Over the next few tortured weeks we talked often by phone. Her mother was against her having a child (she had forced Jen to have two other abortions in her teens). The man in question no longer responded to Jen's phone calls and no one knew where he had gone. His parents loved Jen, but she felt she could not tell them about the situation.

Her inner anguish at the loss of her relationship and having no funds, or health insurance for bringing up a child alone, led her to utmost despair. Another friend had offered to act as father to the child, but he had no funds either and Jen felt that it was unrealistic.

✦

All throughout I watched long distance as the Soul of John, her child to be, went deeper and deeper into the pain of rejection. Jen battled with herself, some days deciding to keep the child, but not knowing how, other days falling into total despair. John's Soul ended up surrounded in darkness and fear. Having committed to be with her, he was now in torment. The same dark cords of fear and loss that had bound them before bound them again, along with the rejection from his father and his grandmother to be, who was actually his mother in this last lifetime. It was so sad to see.

I told Jen I could not advise her to have an abortion knowing all that I knew from her case and from others. Doing so would probably lead to more depression, despair and the loss of a chance to be with John again in this life as her child. I could see that if she would only trust, there was Light at the end of the tunnel. But I was not in a place to tell her to go against her very real financial fears, as she was at that time dependent on loans from her mother, who was strongly against the pregnancy. Jen had been slowly rebuilding her life after the many traumas she had previously seen. There was no money for maternity bills or a hospital birth.

Because of her internal tug of war, I could do nothing other than ask that Christ and the Angels help her with Light and Love until she had made her decision one way or another. It was not my place to make her decision. We both knew the longer she waited the harder it would be for both of them if she decided on an abortion. For me it was a very sad time. The waves of her distress came clear across the ocean. It was not at all surprising to see John sinking into darkness as Jen fought her mother's wishes and her lover's. I understood only too well what Jen was going through. I wished I could have done more for her, but I could only wait, while sending her and John Light and Love.

When Jen decided to go ahead with the abortion, I already knew before she called me. I could see the change in her energy. The fighting was over. She had greyed out. Her energy field was limp and exhausted. Her heart was flat and dark. In her mind she had steeled herself to take action. The arguments of her mother had worn her down.

> "You've made your decision, haven't you?" I asked quietly.
>
> "Yes," she whispered.
>
> "Have you spoken with John?"
>
> "I tried, but I don't think he can hear me anymore," she said in tears.
>
> "I will try to talk to him," I said, "see if I can reach him."
>
> By now I knew his Soul well, but he was so balled up with fear of what was about to happen he reminded me of an inmate on death row. He was hugging his knees, hiding his face, numb with terror in a dark prison of emotional blackness as he awaited his time. He had managed to distance himself somewhat from Jen's field by about ten feet and was floating above her. Yet he was still tethered by the Spiritual cord of Light to his tiny Physical Body, which was bound and tangled by Jen's emotional cords around him.

"John," I said gently, reaching out to him on the inner plane, "Jen doesn't feel she can go ahead with the pregnancy. She loves you and wants the best for you, but she has been abandoned and has no funds. She is desperately sorry."

"I know," John mumbled in pain. His voice seemed far away, strained, tight and bitter.

He was struggling to withdraw his life force and disentangle himself, but her emotional anguish made it very difficult because so much of her Being did not want to let him go. Her mind had been beaten down and was ready to let go, finding no way out, but her heart was not at peace and held on.

I explained to Jen what was happening, that he knew of her decision and was trying to leave, but that she was holding on, stopping him. I led her through the "Forgiveness Prayer" to help her release him and sent Angels to be with them both and to escort John into the Light to be healed when the time came.

✦

In my healing work I cannot take another's life force away from the body. It is not my right to do so. The Angels cannot do this either. We can only assist in transition when a Soul is ready to leave and those left behind are willing to let go. Jen still had a hard time letting go. For all she understood of these things, her heart and mind were not at one. She felt that she had no other option. Her mother said she would have no part in helping support the child, as she had had enough on her hands trying to support Jen through all the turmoil so far in her life. Jen's debts to her mother had become the bargaining chips for John's life. Jen's father was newly wed himself, and Jen felt he was not in a position to help her. Later that day she had the abortion.

✦

Being so sensitive and being given whatever drugs the clinic used, sent Jen into horrendous hallucinations and nausea. Though John did get into the Light safely, he made it clear to me that he would not return as a guide to Jen for at least a year. He needed to get over the shock of it all, especially the rejection. The shock to her body, the drugs she had been given, and the great feelings of loss caused Jen to remain severely depressed for a long time. Unfortunately I could not be with her to help as much as I would have liked due to my being in England at that time.

✦

I finally was able to do a session in person with Jen eleven months later. Jen told me then that the drug "Ultram" that she had been given as a muscle relaxant almost killed her in the clinic, and she had wished that she could die as the abortion proceeded because the hallucinations were so bad. All levels had been affected by the abortion.

Her Higher Self showed a black crack connected to the abortion event and self-destructive tendencies since then. (This had not been there previously, as in our original sessions years ago we had cleared all suicide attempts that would have shown at this level.) The battles with her mother had left a large black hole at Soul level through the heart center.

Jen was not in a good way. We worked through every level clearing the damage. Self-hate had become a major depleting energy in her system. The Emotional and Mental Bodies were both dark and depleted and, along with the Astral Body, showed damage from the drug used in the abortion. The Etheric Body showed massive damage with black holes everywhere, particularly in the head, womb and spine. If not repaired this could easily have become a major illness at the physical level. If no Light is available at the etheric level, cells are depleted at the physical level. The hate towards the man who abandoned Jen and his rejection of her were centered at the sacral chakra, where their energies were still enmeshed. At every level we released other people's energies that had in any way disrupted her life and brought Jen back to balance. It was a big work.

✦

Not long after our session Jen phoned. She was happy again. John had just returned to her side as her guide in Spirit again. It had been almost a year since the difficult events that had separated them.

91

I bless them both and wish them well. Though we live in different places, far away from each other, we stay in touch.

Jen is a gentle Soul extremely sensitive and creative. She has won many awards for her exquisite, colorful creations. Jen's path has not been an easy one, but she is a jewel quietly shining her own Light, and John is excited to help her again with her Sacred designs.

✦

Woman's Heart Problems
Came From Her Grandmother's Desire
to Have Her Aborted

One evening I was giving a lecture on the way love and hate can affect the human energy field. I had specifically said that I would look at people's hearts that day to see how they were functioning, as the heart is so often affected by negative emotions. Lydia, a new person to the class, said she would like a reading to see what I could find.

✦

I checked with Lydia's Guardian Angels and Higher Self (as I always do before giving a reading) to see if we could proceed and was given the O.K., but I was warned to go in gently.

Scanning quickly through her Physical Body, it was clear to me her heart was not functioning normally. I could see arrhythmia immediately. Her heart's energy was dark at cell level, lacking oxygen, as was her brain. Checking the chakras, I found the heart chakras at the front and back of her body were spinning with a negative counter-clockwise spin. At the heart chakra on her back a large dark cleft was apparent, cutting from top to bottom through the heart. Lydia confirmed that she had heart pains regularly, so much so that she could not lie down to sleep but had to sit up in a recliner chair all night. She feared she might die of a heart attack. Pains went down her left arm. She had seen many doctors about her heart, and none knew what was causing the condition.

I then checked all levels of Lydia's Being and found that the dark split showed at every level as far up as Higher

93

Self, her connection to her Source. At that finest level of the human field the split showed as a dark cleft extending from far above her head to down below her feet.

This mark is classic for someone who has been damaged by repeated thoughts of abortion while developing as a fetus. It can also be similar to marks left by a near death experience or a suicide attempt. In this case I felt sure that her mother had considered abortion or was being forced by another to have an abortion and had fought the issue.

I explained what I was seeing, as gently as I could, explaining the implications of such a mark. This is often sensitive ground to cover with a person unknown to me, especially in front of a lecture group. Lydia's response confirmed it all.

"That's amazing Gwen, that you can see that!" she said shocked, "I was told by my mother only two months ago that she had to fight my grandmother to keep me!"

Then Lydia explained what had happened. Her mother, Sarah, was not married and only eighteen when she got pregnant. Lydia's father skipped town as soon as he heard Sarah was pregnant and has never acknowledged Lydia or contacted her since. Lydia's grandmother, Margaret, was pregnant herself at the time and very angry with her daughter for getting pregnant as well as with the young man who abandoned her. Margaret was sure he would never return. She felt it was best for Sarah to have an abortion. They had argued terribly about it. Margaret treated Sarah very harshly and would not let her eat at the family table during her pregnancy. She had to eat alone in her room. Sarah was very angry with her mother and did what she could to protect the baby in her womb. Throughout the pregnancy Margaret had berated Sarah and rejected Lydia. The immense damage done Lydia in gestation showed clearly now in her adulthood. There was a severe reduction in her life force that caused her heart to suffer. She feared sudden death, understandably, as from day one her life had been threatened.

"I loved Grandma," said Lydia, "I couldn't believe that she had not wanted me. Mom said that once Grandma saw me she loved me. I grew up with her own daughter, my aunt, like a sister."

Once Lydia was born, even though her grandmother's heart had changed towards her and she had loved Lydia from that day on, the damage was done. Could Margaret ever have known what damage she had caused? I doubt it. All her loving could not now change the severe attack on the child's life energy field that was done as this tiny embryo was being formed. Imprints such as this go very deep into the DNA and affect every living cellular structure as it is first formed. These then replicate the same message throughout life unless they are consciously reprogrammed.

I led Lydia through the "Forgiveness Prayer" with her mother, grandmother and father. None of these family members were physically present, but I called each one into our Sacred space at Spirit level to do the work. Working with Christ, Mary and the Angels at long distance we did the cleanup. We retrieved as much of Lydia's energy that day as we could and brought her into as much balance as possible in the short time we had available at the lecture.

✦

Lydia subsequently came to see me for private sessions, and we began more in-depth healing work clearing the wounds at all levels. She had many other issues to clear, but this one event, the fight for her life as a fetus, had left a huge mark on her. It was a resonating field that would inevitably reproduce itself again and again until it was changed. As we worked through all the levels of her Being to heal that wound, I found that sixty percent of her life force at Inner Child level was still trying to stop her grandmother's abortion commands. Here was a tiny fetus trying to protect herself by pushing her grandmother's negative energy away. Meanwhile her grandmother's energy was locked around Lydia's Inner Child still trying to prevent her from being born. Lydia's mother had tried to protect her by placing an energetic cocoon around her, which now in Lydia's adult life was stifling her progress. Her father's energy also impacted her and blocked her Inner Child and many other levels.

All these negative energies were transmuted and returned to whomever had created them. Meanwhile, we retrieved Lydia's energy and brought her back into balance. Each step of the way her field became brighter.

In her own adult life Lydia had married and become pregnant only to have her husband abandon her for another woman when her daughter was only seven days old. The abandonment, rejection and fear of an early death theme was locked deep into Lydia's DNA. It was there that we went to clear the imprint.

I found that Lydia's DNA was fighting itself. It was also fighting the negative imprints of everyone that had impacted her, including her husband. These imprints we removed with the help of Christ and the Angels. Once that was done, tremendous strength came back to her. Now it was time for her to reprogram her own life's direction. Fear represses the heart and can reverse the heart chakra spin to a negative counter-clockwise depleting cycle. Love and joy open it up and can correct the spin.

✦

Lydia is progressing and now knows to meditate and to consciously change any old fears into new positive visions for the future. She is creating a new life based on love, not fear. Lydia is a wonderful woman with special healing gifts of her own to bring to the world that she is only now realizing in her Being. In her working life she is a great teacher watching over a whole school of young children.

✦

We may never know how a child will turn out when we conceive. One thing is for sure, if love surrounds that child as he or she is growing in the womb and in the early formative years, love can be the keynote for life.

✦

Did a Pregnant Young Woman's Suicide Attempt Replay her Mother's Thoughts of Abortion?

A young woman was lying in a hospital bed with stab wounds on her chest when my mother called me with the news. It was a family friend. It was not a good situation, as the young woman was also pregnant. My mother asked if I could help, so I sent in Angels and did prayer work, but could do no more without formal permission from the young woman. I did what I could to stabilize her energetically with the help of the Angels.

✦

I witnessed this case from long distance. I was in Texas and the young woman was in England from a family known to me. In talking with her mother she felt that her daughter would probably not accept Spiritual counseling at the time, having been placed under psychiatric care and sedation.

However, the case was of interest to me as I had known this young woman when she was a child, though I had not seen her in many years. She was the last child born to Sue, one of my mother's best friends. I remember well when I was about twelve years old how my mother had told me that Sue was very upset to be pregnant again. Sue was in her mid forties, thinking that she had done with all that came with looking after babies, when suddenly here was an unexpected fourth child on the way. My mother was very worried about Sue, who had wept for days and was considering abortion. In the end Sue changed her mind and went ahead with her pregnancy.

When her daughter April was born, she was a sweet little Soul, gentle and shy. Her brothers and sister were all in their teens by then. Years later her mother confided in me that she couldn't imagine being without this sweet little girl and was sorry she had ever thought otherwise. She said April was the best gift she had ever had.

Many years later, I received word that April had married a foreigner she had met on vacation. It was not an easy marriage due to their cultural differences. It came as a great shock to me now though, to hear that she had tried to commit suicide by stabbing herself in the chest while in the first trimester of her first pregnancy.

✦

Immediately my mind went back to the turmoil I knew Sue had gone through during her pregnancy with April. I wondered if the hormonal shift in April's body with her pregnancy had catalyzed at a deep level of her Being the memories of abortion images imprinted by Sue in the same trimester in her pregnancy. April had not been attempting to take her child's life directly. In stabbing at her chest it was her own life that she was trying to end, though obviously her child would have died also if she had succeeded. Could the chemical messengers related to all that goes with pregnancy have triggered the embedded thought form that impelled her to try to take her own life?

I was fairly sure this was what had happened. Thought forms can stay imprinted for a lifetime, and through centuries, when passed down through the DNA of generations.

April was found and stabilized fairly quickly after her suicide attempt. She did eventually give birth, by all accounts, to an apparently healthy child. Though I have wondered to myself since, how much the imprint from Sue's thoughts of abortion affecting the DNA of April, now affects the DNA of April's own child. He may have a similar death imprint from what happened in both his own life most recently and from April's when she was in the womb.

✦

The dark split I witnessed at Higher Self level in April was the classic mark of one whose mother considered abortion and also of a person who has attempted suicide.

However, as I scanned the situation, I also saw at that time that April's husband had a harsh unyielding energy towards her, which may well have compounded the situation and led to the event going out of control.

✦

I believe it is important for all of us to clear the negative programs running in the background of our lives. For this reason it is vital to know the conditions surrounding us during our gestation and early childhood so that we can heal them.

✦

Abortion Affects a Husband's Heart

When a man and a woman marry but have different ideas about having children, it causes deep rifts in the marriage. For this reason, it is wise for both to agree ahead of time what the outcome of the marriage should be in relation to children. It is unwise to marry with the idea of changing the spouse's mind, or forcing a pregnancy if it is not wanted. There can be nothing sadder than a woman desperate for a child with a husband who does not want children, or a man whose destiny it is to have many children to be with a woman who wants none.

There can be many reasons for not wanting a child. Some may be factors from this lifetime's experience, some from previous lifetimes. Sometimes agreements are made with the best of intentions, but the marriage begins to falter for one reason or another, leaving behind unfinished karma with incoming children who are expecting birth.

Maria, a nurse in her late forties, had come to see me alone about difficulties she was having in her marriage. Her life plan had originally included three children, as had her husband Joe's, but this was not the way things had unfolded. She loved Joe and married him because he was a hard worker, intelligent and a good provider. She had wanted security to raise a family. They had dated for five years, but their plans for children began to go wrong just before the wedding.

Maria and Joe loved to party and drink a lot. Maria had wanted to slim down for the wedding so had been on prescription diet drugs for three months before the wedding. They regularly had drunken weekends. Maria had no idea that she was already pregnant during that period of time she was so out of touch with her body.

We began our session by clearing the difficult abortion that she had had as a result of this unplanned pregnancy. One month into her marriage, four and a half months into the pregnancy, the abortion had been against her wishes. Joe greatly feared that the diet drugs Maria had been using while pregnant might have affected the fetus. Her heavy drinking at the time and how it may have affected the child was also a concern. He had threatened to leave their new marriage if she did not acquiesce to the abortion. He did not want a damaged child. She felt pressured into the abortion to save her new marriage.

Joe did not accompany Maria to the clinic. She went alone and had no support from him during the procedure, even though he was the one who had pushed for it. When the surgeon showed Maria the ultrasound of the child and had told her the child's head was large, she had chosen to believe that he meant the child was damaged. Now, with hindsight, she realized that what he was saying was that the child was more developed than she had first thought. She really had no idea how long she had been pregnant.

The child's body and Soul were very damaged by the act of abortion, and he was enraged with his parents. He had been trapped between the worlds and unable to leave, and his Soul was locked in around her womb energetically. When he demanded to know why his parents had chosen to abort him, Maria had answered that they thought the drugs she had used had damaged him. Neither she nor Joe had realized he had a conscious Soul that could be hurt. She was very sorry for what had happened. With prayers we were able to do the necessary healing and forgiveness for all of them, disentangling the dark emotional cords that bound them. The child's Soul then was able to reach the Light.

This difficult beginning within the first month of their marriage, along with their drinking habits, led to an eventual destruction of their dreams for a happy family with three children.

✦

Maria told me that she had tried to put this abortion behind her, but it was obvious to me that it had left her very wounded until our healing work had been done in this session. Both she and Joe had suffered greatly at many levels as a result of the abortion, but they had been unconscious of how deeply they had been affected.

Eventually, they did have two other children. The first was a child they planned together. He was premature at thirty-two weeks. The second child would have been premature as well if Maria had not taken bed rest from the thirty-second week through to delivery. Maria had felt pressured by Joe into having this child before she was ready. She felt tired and wanted to rest before being pregnant again. She was also beginning to worry about the relationship and was not happy about being pregnant this time.

✦

After an abortion the womb can be left in a depleted state, especially if it is still entangled with the lost child's Soul. An abortion can also leave the body with a hormonal imbalance and low progesterone levels. When progesterone is low, miscarriage or premature birth can occur. Low progesterone also causes tiredness and depression. These factors may have had something to do with Maria's premature births, but also Maria continued to drink at least one or two beers every day during both pregnancies. She thought that this intake was light compared to what she had done in the past and that it would be O.K. In checking with the Angels of the first-born child, I was told that alcohol poisoning was the main factor in this baby's premature arrival. The doctor attending the birth of the second child had commented that the placenta was very calcified and thin and could not easily have nourished the child.

By the time the second child arrived, the marriage was already beginning to flounder. Maria said that their drinking was causing real problems. Doubts about the marriage led Maria to not want any more children with Joe. Yet, she kept trying to please him in order to make the marriage work. She was brought up as a Southern Baptist and felt divorce was out of the question.

> "You know something is wrong with your marriage when you have to drink to get sexually aroused," she said with a sigh.

> "I knew back then that things were badly wrong. I got to the place that I didn't want him to touch me when he was drunk, but I kept giving in to him."

When Maria became pregnant again with what would have been their third child, she decided to have an abortion without telling Joe. She felt she had no energy left for giving birth and rearing another child in their difficult marriage. She did not want to face what Joe might have to say about it. So, in secret, at about five to six weeks into the pregnancy, she had an abortion. Joe did not even know she was pregnant. Things did not go smoothly with the abortion, however, and Joe found out. He was extremely upset about it.

This last abortion left Maria feeling hollow and unable to respond with any desire towards Joe. From this point on, their marriage was effectively over. Since that time over fifteen years had passed. Maria and Joe had stayed together because of their two living children and, unknowingly, because of the karma that silently bound them to the two aborted children.

✦

As I continued the healing work for Maria, I called in the presence of her husband Joe's Spirit after getting permission from his Guardian Angels and Higher Self. I wanted to see how this last abortion had affected both of them in order to take the corrective healing measures now that the first one had been cleared. As Joe approached our healing circle, I could see that the most recent abortion had left a great wound in his heart center in the Emotional Body which was now causing strain on the Physical Body. There was a possibility of an aneurysm because of that strain. Maria confirmed that Joe had heaviness in his chest and that he also suffered from asthma, a classic condition of stifled emotion. Joe's Inner Child stood at his heart center and was holding a tiny coffin in his hands. The Inner Child was very sad and depleted.

This healing work included the disentangling of years of bitterness between Maria and Joe along with the release of this last aborted child's Soul from both of them. Maria and Joe were broken at many levels from their battles with one another, particularly at the heart level and at sexual areas where the energy was severely depleted.

In working with Maria on her Physical Body, we cleared her womb of the effects of the most recent abortion. It had left a dark twisted energy in her system from her womb to her head. No wonder all desire had gone. There was no energy left for her to have feelings at that level.

103

We used the "Forgiveness Prayer" between Maria and Joe
and the child's Soul so that each could forgive the other
and to clear the dark cords that bound them. Once the
child's Soul was released, she was clearly a much-loved
Spiritual friend of Joe's from a past life. This is why it
had caused him so much grief and pain. With the first
abortion, Joe had really believed he was doing the right
thing, because he thought the child might already have
been damaged. Though the first one had depleted his
energy badly, it was this last abortion that had broken his
heart. He had always wanted a daughter.

Maria could now see that it had been her husband's destiny to have
this child, but sadly it had been Joe's own abusive behavior that had led
Maria to have the last abortion. Joe was probably unconscious of his part
in the destruction of something he so dearly wanted. Alcohol had made
him blind to his family's needs. He had lost his Spiritual direction and
forgotten his agreements with his wife and children.

Maria had given up drinking some years prior to seeing me in this
session, but Joe's pattern had remained much the same. Alcohol had
played a major role in the destruction of this family where children had
originally been wanted.

With this knowledge and the healing work that was done at every level
of her Being, Maria became much more balanced. She finally let go of all
of her anger towards her husband. She also forgave herself. Now, with the
clearing work completed, she could see much more of what had kept their
broken relationship hobbled together and what part each had played.

As they received back their own Spiritual energies, I could see Joe's
heart had begun to brighten considerably on all levels, even though he was
miles away. Once the work was done, the Angels returned Joe's Spirit to
his body and took the child's Soul into the Light. Maria's own energy was
back and she could now make her choices based on a new reality.

✦

A Century's Old Curse
Behind Eight Abortions.

Christina's whole Being was beaten down when she arrived at my door. She was in her mid fifties, yet looked like a thin waif of a child with long unruly hair down her back. Her clothes hung on her bony frame like laundry blowing on a line, as if nothing fit right. It was as though her whole life did not fit her. Neither her clothes, nor her body, nor her Spirit fit her. She was not fully present in this world.

She told me she wanted purification and a better understanding about the problems of her marriage.

Although she actually stood taller than I, her demeanor was pale and shrunken, with a diminutive frightened air that made her seem tiny and frail. It was as if a great weight hung about her shoulders, which indeed it did on the inner plane. She was weighed down with guilt, shame and exhaustion within a marriage where she had no voice.

There was much to be done, so much to work through to bring Christina's Spirit back. The reason I have included just one fragment of her story here is because it may provide an important key to someone reading this book.

✦

Not all events in our present life have their beginning in this time. Sometimes a past life can cause such damage that it reverberates through to the present.

A key event for Christina happened in France many centuries ago. The impact was so great, she was still reeling and reacting to it, yet she did not know it.

When I asked my guides where we should begin to heal Christina, I was taken straight to her DNA. There I found that her life was being literally pulled apart by a repeating negative energy pattern. Tracking into the darkness to the tearing down that was happening at DNA level, I found a link to her life in twelfth-century France.

The first image that came was of Christina's own suicide while pregnant. She was wearing the vestments of a nun. She lay on a grassy bank in a pool of her own blood by a moat that was overshadowed by a dark grey stone castle. The Mother Superior of her convent had found the body and was very angry. There was no sympathy for Christina. This was something to be hidden and covered up. Christina's body was subsequently buried without last rites in unsanctified ground. Suicide was considered an unholy act.

A large part of Christina's Soul was trapped there, as was the Soul of her unborn child. Neither had known any rest.

I asked my guides to take me back to the beginning of that life to see what had transpired to make Christina choose such an action. I found that in her late teens she had been very happy and in love with a young man, but that her father was angry at the relationship and had Christina put away in the nunnery against her wishes. The young man continued to see her secretly. Eventually he joined the military. His troop was sent south to a battle where he was killed. Christina had just realized she was pregnant when news came of his death. This was devastating to her, as the love they had was true; however, this was not the reason for her suicide. The Mother Superior, on finding that Christina was pregnant, called her a whore and cursed her for her evil ways, damming her to certain hell for what she had done to bring disgrace upon the order. This is what had tipped the balance for Christina, and she felt it was better to die and be with her lover than live without him in shame. Sadly she understood little of what happens in suicides, and how easily one can become trapped between the worlds. The combination of the Mother Superior's curse and her own grief held a large part of her Being still trapped in that time.

+

As the story became clear, Christina wept tears and sobbed with great grief.

"Oh, Gwen," she sobbed, " do you think that curse went so deep as to affect my thinking now in this life?"

106

"Without a doubt, the program is running at DNA level," I said, "one of self destruction."

"Is that perhaps the reason that so many times I did not want a child in this life?" she asked.

"The damage and imprint is very dark around that issue," I said. "It would have a great impact, yes."

"Gwen," she cried out loud as if needing absolution right then, "I HAD EIGHT ABORTIONS IN THIS LIFE! All between ages twenty one to thirty two!"

With this her grief came like a howling, soughing wind, a sobbing and wailing from centuries of pain. It was as if all the Souls of her lost children wept with her.

I called in extra Angels and the Christ Light to stabilize all those needing help to begin the healing work. There was a flurry of wings and Light in all directions. Peace began to return to the room.

✦

I gave Christina a few drops of the Bach Flower essence called "Rescue Remedy," in a glass of water to stabilize her and suggested she take just a few sips as we worked. This remedy will help balance a person when in great distress, yet it is a gentle remedy that can be bought over the counter in any health store.

Christina began to calm down and told me her story in full.

She had only one child in this life with the husband that she had married when she was in her late twenties. The last abortion was at his command and was the thing that had finally broken her in this life. She had been raised Catholic. She could tell no one about what had happened. No one in her family knew. Until now, she had suffered alone with this burden. Her body showed the classic scars of a suicide in a past life. The break showed up as a dark slash at Higher Self level. Her sexual area, womb, liver and the base of her spine at the root chakra all showed great damage linked to these events.

✦

We began the big cleanup by first going back to the time of her death in the twelfth century. I went in with the Angels, Christ and Mary. We used the "Forgiveness Prayer" between her and all the individuals involved with her in that life, including her lover, father, the Mother Superior and the child. We made sure all got their rightful energy back, blessed in Christ Light. Most importantly, we removed the curse. Then we took Christina's Soul, her child's Soul and the Soul of her lover who had died on that distant field into the Light. This way I could be certain that all necessary healing was completed in that lifetime. I always ask the Angels to take newly-passed Souls to the first level of Heaven (where they should return immediately following death), for complete healing before going further on into the Light.

Once Christina was healed and her completions were done with her lover and with their child, I brought her back to this life from the Light. She was much brighter and her heart was more at peace, as she had retrieved a large part of her energy back from her lost love.

I asked the Angels to take the child's Soul and Christina's lover's Soul to wherever they needed to be in this lifetime, if they currently had a Physical Body. This way the Angels can help them reintegrate what is theirs, provided it is according to God's Holy Law. Sometimes people are not ready to receive their Light back. The Angels know what to do and will work with the Guardian Angels of the people in question, so I leave that work up to them.

Then I requested that the whole area that had been the scene of such sadness be purged in God's Light to remove any residual difficulties. Once I saw this was done, I closed that doorway in space and time, bringing myself back to the present.

✦

Next, we moved to take care of the abortions in this lifetime. We used the same "Forgiveness Prayer" to clear all these Souls and release them into the Light. As we did so, we retrieved Christina's energy purified as Christ

Light, and we returned energy as Christ Light to others involved.

Thought forms of self-hate and anger towards her husband were then cleared from the base of the spine, sacral area and liver. The darkness from her anger at her husband about the last abortion was locked up in her sexual area and had led to a variety of infections. We worked on clearing these by using the "Forgiveness Prayer" once again, and by working with her husband long distance on the inner plane. He had thoroughly controlled her Being through her sexual center and her Mental Body. Once this controlling energy was removed, Christina's own life energies came back into those areas and she became herself.

We then cleared the break at Higher Self level, so that her life force could flow in more easily.

+

Staphysagria would be a key remedy for Christina to help her get over the abortions and find her voice again in her marriage, where she had felt completely overpowered. She had been brought up in a very difficult family situation. As the youngest of many, she had never really found her voice at that time, and had always tended to give in to those in authority. Now, her energy was back from this difficult French lifetime, and she was much stronger, more present, and better able to stand up for her own needs.

+

A curse can go deep and affect every fiber of our Being. Unfortunately, the harshness of the beliefs in the twelfth century have not changed much. This is a lesson for every person. If you curse another, and damn them to hell for simply being pregnant out of wedlock, your voice may reverberate for centuries to come.

Did the Mother Superior also suffer for her words? Indeed she did, for it was her own life force she had used to bind Christina in that hateful hell. Therefore, until now, she had also locked part of her own Being in the same hell Christina had been assigned to.

✦

Christina had a few days with me. We continued working at all levels of her being clearing many other issues. She left a different woman, radiant and strong with her DNA pattern now one of abundant life, not self-destruct and self-hate. She was ready for a new creative life.

✦

Aversion to Pregnancy Comes from Past Life Death in Childbirth

Maggie was angry and bitter about the way things had gone in her marriage. Everything had broken down badly. There was a huge rift between her and her husband and their two children. The marriage seemed to have gone to a place of no return.

Maggie is a strong, healthy woman in her forties who is also very attractive. When she came to see me, however, she was looking drawn, sad, and worn out with all the fighting in her family. She no longer knew how to find the love she sought with her husband, Frank, and more particularly, she never seemed to have found it with her two teenage children.

The children, a boy and a girl, had become the brunt of the arguments between Maggie and Frank, and now the children were either arguing with Maggie or just ignoring her. She did not know how to reach them. She felt cut off from their world. From the beginning she had not been able to bond with them.

✦

I asked Maggie if she had really wanted children. She told me she had never really had the desire to bring children into the world, that it was Frank who had wanted kids.

"I never even played with dolls as a child. The truth is, all I wanted was my horses. They were all I knew," said Maggie.

"Why did you marry Frank if he wanted children and you didn't really want them?" I asked.

"Oh," she sighed. "We were dating and I got pregnant by accident. I was on the pill, it shouldn't have happened. It took us both by surprise, but we agreed that getting married was the best thing to do. Frank was a good guy and came from a good family. He really wanted to have the child and we cared about each other. I was in my early thirties at the time and all of my friends were telling me I shouldn't miss out on having a family. I thought maybe they could be right. I just didn't know for sure."

"All the marriage plans went ahead, but I miscarried before the wedding. Even though I miscarried, we decided to get married anyway."

"How did you feel about being pregnant at first?" I asked.

"I didn't know what to feel. I guess I was ambivalent. It just happened," she replied.

"I guess I really didn't want to be pregnant; I hadn't planned it. I just didn't know what to do. I worried about being pregnant. I just didn't have that nurturing, motherly urge that seems to make other women want to have kids. It just wasn't there in me. Though I knew how to take care of kids as far as feeding and clothing them went, I honestly didn't know what to do with them."

"I told Frank that if he wanted kids, he would have to learn to look after them. I didn't want to be the only caregiver. I really only wanted my horses."

She explained that her husband had done his part in taking care of the kids as he had agreed from early on. He was now taking them to all the ball games, the practices, the extra-curricular activities, etc. It was non-stop. He really had done a good job with them, and Maggie agreed she could not complain. But she said they were always away without her.

Their lives had gone in different directions early in the marriage a few years after the children were born. Father and kids had gone one way; she and the horses, the other. The family never included her in their plans now. Even though she cooked for them, she never knew their schedules. She felt left out and sad, spending all her time with her horses, alone.

She said she did not know how to love or bond with her children. She wanted to feel love between them. Something was missing in her heart.

"I guess I know how to love my horses more than my kids," she sighed.

Her pregnancies with her children had gone well enough, even though both had gone two weeks beyond full term and were cesarean sections.

"They just didn't seem to want to be born," said Maggie.

Was it their wishes or her fears that had held them back, I wondered to myself.

✦

The first pregnancy was her son. He was born jaundiced and had to spend three days in an incubator. She was not allowed to touch him and could not bond easily afterwards. Her son in particular bore a lot of anger towards her now. He was almost fourteen. Maggie had not been able to bond with her daughter either, yet both children had bonded well with their father. Looking at their past life connections, I could see both children previously had good lives with their father, so that bonding had come easily to them. Maggie had had one minor dispute in a past life with her son over a land deal. We cleared this up quickly, but it was not the key to her story.

I felt that her lack of desire to have children and to bond with them went beyond Maggie's present life experience. It seemed to me that below the surface a much deeper current was running. Her lack of ability to feel motherly love for her children told me some major part had been cut off from her Being. This situation was not so much about a lack of love between her and Frank, because in spite of their arguments, there seemed to be genuine affection on her part towards him at some level as she spoke to me about him. No, the block was more about being pregnant, and even more than that about the birth process itself, which she had managed to delay by two weeks in both cases.

✦

The first step was to check on the miscarriage. I located the Soul of the child, who would have been a girl had

113

she been born. The child had chosen to leave because she could sense the ambivalence and worry in Maggie. Though Maggie did not remember trying to speak with the child's Soul directly, or ask her to leave, she did remember feeling very worried about the situation.

We did forgiveness work with Maggie, the child's Soul and her husband Frank at long distance using the "Forgiveness Prayer." Then I made sure that each of them got their energy back in the pure form as Christ Light. A sad cloud lifted from Maggie as this was done. I could see it also lifted a weight off Frank. Once all was cleared, the Angels took the child's Soul into the Light. Because this had been a fairly early term miscarriage, and the child had chosen to leave, there was no apparent damage to the child's Soul. In fact, the child said she was sorry to have caused them any discomfort and that she would like to return one day in the future as a guide for Maggie.

The child's Soul was not trapped by any violence done to her, but by sadness of loss from both parents, particularly Frank, which had not allowed her to retrieve all of her energy from the situation until now, so she had been unable to go fully into the Light.

✦

Still, this was just a beginning. I felt that this miscarriage was the result of a deeper fear in Maggie. Now it was time to track it back to its origins. I found that there was more than just one lifetime that had affected Maggie in a negative way around her sexuality. The most important one, however, and the one that held the key to childbirth, began in Scotland a long time ago.

✦

When I asked my guides to take me back to the beginning of Maggie's problems, the first image I was given was a dark bloody mass on a black and green tartan spread. The blood was fresh. I found myself in a small, stone, crofter's cottage. It was dark and damp inside this one-room cottage. There was no fire in the hearth, only grey ash and no light, except what seeped under the ill-fitting wooden door and through a small window high up in the wall under the reed-thatched roof. Outside a miserable

114

wet mist was creeping over the peat moor. There was a woman alone on a wooden cot, hemorrhaging and in great pain as she tried to give birth. The baby could not leave her body, as it was locked in her pelvis. She and the child died. This was Maggie in a previous life who had labored so tragically alone. It is no wonder that now, in this life, she had no desire to give birth.

Yet there was more to this story. As I began to lift the child's Soul in that time from her womb, I found the child had a terrible vengeance in his eyes from a previous life. This was no ordinary child who had died inside her. They had battled in a previous life as well. It was in that previous life that this whole painful sequence was set in motion.

Following the child's eyes back to his previous violent death scene, I found myself in a battle raging between Romans and Barbarians in the borderlands between what is now Scotland and England. All hell was breaking loose as armies clashed. The child's Soul was now that of a powerfully built, crudely-dressed, Barbarian. He had an unkempt matted beard, wild eyes and long hair. His fury knew no bounds. He cursed with every slash of his short dagger as he fought the Romans through the treacherous boggy lowland. Opposing him came a tall Roman striking a fearful blow that caught the Barbarian square in the side of the head. The Barbarian reared up in blinding pain, screaming and cursing the man to hell as he slashed out at the Roman's neck.

The Roman did not die instantly. As the Barbarian sank down to the ground holding onto his adversary, his eyes bore a hatred and a curse that would stay locked in the Roman's Soul forever. Their Spirits were locked together in that death scene and were still tearing at one another.

When Maggie became pregnant in the next life centuries later, it was this Barbarian's avenging Spirit that took hold as her child. He was still seeking to fulfill his curse to kill the Roman soldier, the same Spirit who was now Maggie. They died together again that bitter day, locked in pain in a thwarted birth.

This was what had blocked all desire for children in Maggie.

✦

Although in this life Maggie had had her battles with her children and husband, none of them were in any way a part of the Barbarian's Spirit. Neither had the Soul of the child who had miscarried in this life been this vengeful Being.

The Barbarian's Spirit was still locked up in Maggie's Being in this lifetime, but he had not attempted to become her child again. Why? Because he died cursed by his own actions. Much of his life force was lost in that distant time. Their battles had continued in the Spirit worlds all those years back in time. No wonder Maggie was ambivalent about having her children and could not bond with them. So much had been taken from her in that previous life that she was not fully present in this life and had nothing much to give.

It made perfect sense that she had opted for cesarean sections after all the long wait for delivery. She did not want to face another painful death. There was no way in this lifetime, with her narrow hips, she could have an easy delivery, and with the added terror of that last life, I doubt that even if she had been graced with big hips could she have been encouraged to go for a normal delivery.

✦

I broke the release work into three sections starting with the first battle scene, clearing the curse and healing the wounds. Using the "Forgiveness Prayer" between Maggie (the Roman) and the Barbarian we began the healing process. I also included all others who had died in that battle in our prayers. This is something I do when I find battles that have left terrible damage behind. I request that at least two Angels are available for every Soul on the field needing help, and we take all Souls into the Light, en masse, who may have become trapped in that time. I do not distinguish between sides in battles, as I know we have all fought so many times in so many guises it would be foolhardy to say one side was right and one side wrong. It is not for me to judge. I do know that Souls who are damaged need help. I leave it up to the Angels to do the healing work at the first level of Heaven where there are many wonderful healers working. They then return these Souls to wherever they belong once they are healed.

> After we had taken the Barbarian's Soul and Maggie as the Roman into the Light in that lifetime, I waited for them to be perfectly healed before moving them onward. Once that lifetime was cleared, I asked that Christ Light purge the field of battle removing all residual sadness, grief or other negative emotions. Then I closed that time doorway down.

> Bringing their Souls forward in time from Heaven, we did a clearing for their deaths in the cottage and took both of them into the Light again in that life, for complete healing. Once again, I asked that Christ Light purge the scene, and I closed that time doorway down.

> The Angels brought Maggie's Soul back from the first level of Heaven to her body in this life completely whole from all wounds she had received in those two lives. The Barbarian's Soul remained at the first level in the Light.

> I then requested that all residual energies relating to the Barbarian that had affected Maggie or her family members in this life be cleared. Then the work was complete. The Barbarian's Spirit was free to go on to new lives. His karma and Maggie's were now complete.

Maggie's life force returned strongly into her Being that day. Much of her energy had been locked in time in those two difficult lives so many centuries ago. It had taken so much of her Being she could not be fully present for her children. Though this was just one small part of resolving the issues with her family, it explained a great deal to her.

✦

Now she could live free of the curse that had stopped her from being able to bond with her children and fully love them.

✦

When a Child Dies

There have been many stories written about near-death experiences. We tend to think of these events as somewhat miraculous, but they are actually very common. What *is* miraculous is the effect these experiences can have upon the Soul of the person who returns, and the way it impacts their entire belief system. But what happens if that person is very young and has no one with whom to corroborate the experience?

Many years ago I lived in a shared apartment with a roommate called Francisco, who was from Peru. We had an interesting friendship based on mutual respect and a wide-ranging interest in different Spiritual philosophies. We were not in a relationship, and he had many different women friends. He had been divorced for some time. On occasion his ex-wife and eight year old daughter would come for a visit.

Francisco had been accustomed to great wealth in Peru, but after the political changes there, much of the family lands had been taken over by the government and given to communes.

His ex-wife was from a very wealthy family in California, a millionairess who was always in a hurry and was wound up like a tight spring. She was clearly not a happy woman, and although sharply dressed, she was aggressive in her manner at all times. She had all the trappings of wealth and had instilled in their daughter disrespect for anything not high-priced. Her high spending was what had driven her husband into bankruptcy, as he just could not keep up. He had built fine hotels in the area but lost his construction business due to her high credit card debt, which she continued to run up in his name even now. She was out of control. He had stopped working completely for two years and had turned to drink. Now he was pulling himself back together, but the marriage had failed in horrible arguments, which the child had witnessed.

Their daughter, Catherine, asked me one day where I bought my clothes. I told her I made most of them, but otherwise I bought locally at any shop when I could afford it. She said that *they* only bought at Neiman Marcus and why on earth would I make my clothes? Only poor people did that. I smiled and told her that sewing was an art, and I chose to make my own dresses because I wanted to be special and different from other folks in what I wore. I had been taught dressmaking at school and even made my own fully tailored tweed coat at age sixteen. I told her I was glad I could sew. It was fun. She said that nobody had taught her to sew, though the nuns at school had attempted to teach her to knit on big needles, but she didn't like it.

"Perhaps one day you would like to learn to sew," I had said.

Outside she had a large doll's house on the deck where she would play. One day after her mother had left, I sat with Catherine and her father and made a small play dough dog for her to put in the doll's house. She took it and squashed it flat. I took it back gently and said that was no way to treat a special little dog, and I reformed it. Her father admonished her and told her she should receive the gift kindly. She put the dog to the side of the house out of view.

Inside her doll's house everything was in chaos. No order. Beds were unkempt and things thrown everywhere. Dolls were upside down on their heads. Chairs were up-turned and dishes turned over on the floor. One small toy mouse sat amidst the clamor. I remarked how nice it was to have such a fine big doll's house to play with. She told me her father had made it for her. It was special.

I said nothing about the chaos inside but could only guess it was the family represented in all its sadness and rage.

✦

Some weeks later I overheard Francisco having a conversation on the phone with his ex-wife. He was concerned about his daughter, who had become disruptive at school again. The nuns were threatening to have her taken out of the school. They were talking about psychiatrists and sedating her with some form of drug. I was horrified at what I was hearing. This child clearly had problems, but none that drugs would resolve.

I asked Francisco what it was about. He said she had become uncontrollable at the Catholic school and was throwing tantrums. At that time, I had not formally begun my healing work, but I knew there was something that needed to be done, and fast. I asked Francisco to have Catherine visit us and I would talk with her, if he would approve. He was not sure it could help, but he was open to anything at that moment.

On her next visit, she came into my room and was admiring the small crystals on my altar. I told her they were special for healing work. She was always fascinated by the artwork I had in my room and the different projects I was working on, but there was always an edge to her, an agitated jumpiness.

Today she asked me what my meditation cushions were for. I told her that I meditated.

"Is that like praying?" she asked.

"Yes it is. It is exactly like that. It is how I get in touch with God," I said.

"Can I do it?" she asked, looking all excited.

"Anyone can," I said. "Here, you sit on these red cushions, and I'll sit on the blue ones." I motioned towards the cushions on the floor.

Immediately she sat and watched me as I sat down and crossed my legs in a half lotus. She did exactly the same.

"Now close your eyes and breathe deeply." I said, "Let your mind go quiet and follow your breathing as it flows in and out of your body."

I was surprised how quickly she calmed from her usual agitated state.

"Breathe in golden Light, Catherine, and let it fill you. This is the Light of Christ, let it fill you up." I said gently, as I too began to go deeper into the calm presence of the

Christ Light. I smiled to myself as I saw how deeply she was going.

"You are a natural meditator Catherine. This is easy for you, isn't it?"

She looked peaceful and smiled with her eyes closed, and nodded completely at ease.

Suddenly there was a knock at the door, making us both jump, and Francisco was peering into the room.

"I have never heard you so quiet. I wondered what you were doing!" he said with a laugh. "I thought you had both vanished into thin air."

"I was teaching Catherine to meditate." I said with a smile, "She's a natural at it."

"Well, lunch is ready," he said, looking at me with a curious grin. "How did you make her so quiet? She's never that quiet? Did you use magic?"

Catherine jumped up off her cushions and ran by us.

"No magic." I said, as she rushed by me, "just Christ Light."

✦

We went into the living room for lunch. Francisco loved to cook and had made a large spaghetti Bolognese. As we sat, I said to Catherine that I would like to have a quiet talk with her and maybe go for a walk.

Her immediate response was, "I'll pass."

"Catherine," I said, "this may be the last time we will have a chance to talk. I will be leaving here shortly and going to another place. You might not see me again. I think it is very important we talk."

"Go on, Catherine," said Francisco. "Go with Gwen. It will give you some fresh air while I clean up."

So, reluctantly at first, she agreed, not knowing what this was all about. We had never spent any real alone time together, so my request probably seemed unusual to her. We walked slowly away from our apartment down toward the little park a few blocks away. After some casual conversation that was going nowhere, I realized I just had to hit home. As we walked, I was asking my guides for the right things to say. I knew for this child it was a critical moment in her life's path. The Angels did not want me let this child go until the healing was done. I had to find where she was damaged.

"Catherine," I asked, "what has hurt you the most in your life?"

To my surprise she answered straight away, without a moment's hesitation.

"There are three things: my mouse just died, my grandfather died last week and Mommy and Daddy don't live together anymore."

"That's a lot," I said. "That's an awful big lot you have had to deal with."

"Let's sit down on this log and talk, shall we?"

I motioned to a fallen oak, but she did not sit for long. She was too full of emotional turmoil, so I followed her as she randomly pulled at dead grass and leaves, weaving her way through the trees and undergrowth.

"That your mouse and your grandfather died, I can't change Catherine, and I am sorry that happened, but the timing of our death is something we can't always argue about. It seems to be in God's hands."

"Let's discuss this all point by point," I said, thinking hard where to begin such a serious talk with one so young.

"First, let's deal with your Mommy and Daddy. What has your Daddy told you about the situation?"

"He says that unless he and Mommy can be friends, they can't live together, but I want them to be together so we can be a family again!" she said full of emotion, but no tears were coming.

She was dried up inside emotionally, overspent with the tides that had swept over her for so many years from her parents' arguments. She was torn in two.

"I know your Daddy loves you dearly and would love for the marriage to have worked. I think he is a very old Soul. He is a wise man and perhaps wants to protect you from seeing such unhappy arguments. He is also a very Spiritual man, and has told me so many times how he loves you more than anything in his life. He does not want to see you hurt. Your Mommy, however, seems to me to be a very young Soul. By that, I mean she has not been here many times on Earth and is not sure how to do the right things for you or for your Daddy."

"I know. You are right," said Catherine. "She is a liar and she drinks. She is horrible to live with. I hate it. She is always lying to Daddy and she lies to me."

I was a little shocked, to say the least, that this eight-year-old would be so forthright about her mother.

"So you understand the difficulty your Daddy faces. He wants for you to be happy, but as he says, if they cannot be friends it only makes matters worse to fight every day."

"Yes, I understand, but I wish I could have my family back together. I miss Daddy. I want them to love each other and me."

"We cannot force that or change it Catherine, but you can still love them."

"Let's talk about your grandfather," I said. "I didn't know he died."

This is what finally began some tears. This child had much to grieve over. She had many losses, and nobody had listened.

"Why couldn't he wait? It was only two days before their wedding anniversary. He could have made it to that. Grandma was so upset," she said in tears.

123

"Sometimes we are called by God, and it may not seem fair to those left behind, but it is our time. Perhaps your grandfather did not want to ruin the memory of the anniversary for your grandma. Death is not a horrible thing when you see it from the point of view of the Spirit leaving. It is a very beautiful thing to go back to God. It is hard for those left behind. We all grieve for the loss of friendship and hugs, but the Spirit is eternal and never really leaves us. Your grandfather is able to be with you in Spirit even now."

She became less agitated. "Do animals go to God when they die?" she asked with her eyes still full of tears. "The nuns said my mouse would not go to Heaven."

"I believe we all go back to God," I said, "and we can return to be with our friends. I often see the Spirit of my old dog around me. She is happy and full of fun. That is the dog I made for you in play dough. Of course I cried when she died. I missed her a lot but she's still with me."

By now we had come to the park swings. She sat on a swing and gently began swinging herself as I broached the next subject, which I knew would be the key.

"But Catherine, you already know all about death, don't you?" I said.

"What happened to you when you were very small?" I asked.

Francisco had told me she drowned at age two. She had been confirmed dead and then been miraculously revived.

"I drowned," she said matter of factly.

The parent swinging a child next to us nervously moved his own child away, with a horrified backward look at us. Catherine was indifferent to his look and continued.

"I was in the house alone with Mommy. We had a pool. She was drinking inside the house and did not pay attention.

I fell in and was screaming but she did not hear me. Then as my body sank to the bottom, I was suddenly floating out of it. I was trying to get her attention. Daddy arrived home. He immediately sensed something was wrong. He asked her where I was. She said I was sleeping and not to disturb me. He knew something was wrong, because I was there beside him screaming at him to find me. He ran to the pool and dove straight in with all his clothes on, and his shoes. He was crying a lot when he got me out. I was dead and had gone a funny blue color. He tried to bring me back by pumping on my chest. Water came out, but I couldn't breathe."

"What happened next?" I asked. "Did you see anything?"

"It was beautiful," she said. "There was such beautiful music, and Light and the Angels came to me and took me to God. It felt so peaceful and warm and loving. I wanted to stay, but they told me I had to go back, that I had not completed what I came to do. They said I must go back and teach the world about God, and that Mommy and Daddy needed me."

"So what happened then?" I asked, fascinated at the detail of her story.

"God had to put a lot of Light into my body to make it possible for me to come back. It was hard for me; it hurt a lot coming back. My body was so stiff and cold and solid after my being dead so long. I remember floating above it and seeing my Daddy there weeping and holding my hand with doctors and nurses all around. Mommy was by the door looking nervous."

"So you came back with a very important mission," I said. "Perhaps you will teach your Mommy and Daddy and that is what you are here for. You can also teach the world about God."

She was hanging upside down on the climbing frame, swinging lightly from her knees. She stopped swinging and twisted her head up to look at me.

"But I have a problem," she said. "My name is Catherine."

"Yes." I said, "Why would that be a problem?"

"There are two Saints by the name of Catherine," she replied. "One heals the sick, the other gives to the poor. Which one am I supposed to be like?"

"I think you have a good chance of being like both." I smiled, "You are the only daughter of a millionairess, and I know for a fact you will be a great healer too."

I took two of the small crystals out of my pocket she had admired earlier. "And in honor of you being a healer, these crystals are for you as a symbol of your new life."

With that her eyes got wide. "They are for me?"

"Yes, I kept them for you, until you were ready."

She leapt to the ground in an acrobatic flip. "I can really keep them?"

"Of course. And I will even show you how to sew a special silk pouch for them when we get back."

✦

With that we headed back home, this time in silence hand in hand. A peace had come about her. She was no longer the fractious child. She was a young woman with a mission.

I taught her how to sew. Her stitches were bendy and not straight at first, but she persevered for about twenty minutes and then disappeared outside onto the deck. I let her go and finished the small pouch for her in white silk, with a gold cord to tie it, and placed the crystals inside.

When I went outside to show her, her doll's house had been put completely in order. Beds were made with each doll in its place. The toy mouse had pride of place and had been given a bowl of play dough food. There next to it sat my play dough dog, now promoted to a position inside the house, with her own bowl of food. I was very touched to see the difference. She explained whose bed was whose. Grandfather was resting on his bed asleep. Her world had become more peaceful. That night when she left and we said our goodbyes, I knew she would not need drugs or a psychiatrist. She was at peace with herself.

✦

That evening I told Fransico what had happened. He was amazed and cried as he recounted his version. Everything she had said fit his story, but amazingly neither parent had ever thought to discuss her drowning with her. They thought she would not remember and had tried to push on without giving her the chance to review this most important event in her life. She had in fact been pronounced dead. Her heart had stopped. Francisco, not believing she would die, told the doctors to try everything they could. They used all the life support equipment they had until a tiny pulse came back, but she was in a coma for two days. Francisco had prayed to God continuously to bring her back. He said he had never gotten over the image of her drowned at the bottom of the pool. It was like a hole in his belly, a darkness in his Emotional Body. It was after this that the marriage had gone so badly wrong. Now the healing could begin for them all.

✦

I did not see Catherine again as I moved away to a new town. In that day it seemed important that our time together was our last. She may not have spoken so openly if she had thought I was to be around. Wherever she is though, I am sure Angels are guiding her on her special mission just as they have guided me, and I bless her on her path. Maybe one day we will meet again.

✦

Abortion after X-ray Exposure, a Child Returns Quickly

Margaret is a very Spiritual woman with a strong understanding of the realms of Spirit. She has four healthy children. As I took notes on her case, I asked her if she had had any miscarriages or abortions she needed to clear. She told me that many years ago she was in a good marriage and was working in a hospital when she became pregnant.

She was unaware of her pregnancy at first and continued her work in the X-ray department. When she realized she was pregnant, her doctors advised her that the X-rays might have damaged the embryo. Reluctantly she agreed to have an abortion, but spoke to the Spirit of the child before doing so, explaining the reason for the decision and welcoming the child's Spirit back as soon as the child wished to be in a new body.

After the abortion, Margaret became pregnant again almost instantly, and felt very strongly that this was the same child coming back to her. The child was born healthy.

✦

As I did the clearing work, there was very little to be done energetically as a result of the abortion. It had been very early term, and the child's Soul had not become entrapped due to her mother's loving concern and communication.

It seemed to me that the child's Soul had been able to leave easily, even before the abortion took place, as Margaret did not entangle her with negative emotions. Instead Margaret had sent the child's Spirit love and lifted her up with Light. As a result the child was able to return as her next pregnancy without a problem.

✦

Talking With a Breech Baby's Spirit Before Birth

Jessica phoned me from England in a panic. Her daughter was about to give birth in Texas and the baby was in a breech position. They had tried to turn him three times, and each time he had turned back to breech.

"Can you see what is happening?" she asked.

"Give me your daughter's full name at birth, her birthdate, and place of birth, so I can track her." I said.

This Jessica did.

"Is there a name for the baby yet?" I asked.

"Dylan Thomas," she said.

"You have got to be kidding me," I laughed, "Dylan Thomas?"

"Yes! They like the name!" she said, a little defensively, though I could tell she was smiling too at the implications.

"Okay, let me see if I can reach them on the inner plane."

Jessica had been a midwife for years, so she knew the complications of a breech birth only too well and was beside herself about not being with her daughter at this time. This would be her first grandchild. She wanted her daughter to have an easy delivery.

✦

I reached her daughter's energy and looked at the child's body. Sure enough he was breech. So I spoke to his Spirit.

"Dylan, your Mom wants you to turn around so you can be born in a normal way, with your head down."

"No way!" came back the reply. "I'm not going to go through all that pain. I want things nice and easy. I want a caesarean."

I told Jessica what he just said. "He says, 'No way.' He wants a caesarian. Doesn't want the pain."

Jessica replied, "Well she wants a natural birth. Tell him that."

This was beginning to seem like a comedy to me. I refocused on Dylan away from his Granny-to-be in England, who was getting all hot and bothered on the other end of the phone.

"Okay Dylan, your Granny says your Mom wants a natural birth. Can you oblige?"

I swear that kid's Spirit winked at me.

"Nope," he said, "I want to come in with all my Spiritual gifts intact. No way am I going down that birth canal!"

He was not angry, just emphatic as if he found it all very amusing. He seemed to be fully enjoying the situation. I would even go so far as to say he was smug and loved the position of control he was in. I sensed he had his arms crossed, leaning back grinning at the world in peaceful bliss. He knew exactly what he wanted and was not going to budge.

"Sorry." I said to Jessica, "No deal. He won't budge. I suggest you line up a caesarean. What do you expect with a name like Dylan Thomas? This guy does not want to budge, and he doesn't want to lose his Spiritual smarts by crushing his head down that birth canal. And that's that, I'm afraid."

Jessica laughed, "I figured he would be a Spiritual type coming from Delilah. Well, I will tell her what you said. She is probably going to wait another few days. She's determined to go natural, but if he doesn't turn, they will have to do a C-Section. He is too big in the position he is in. I'll let you know."

"This guy is going to be a handful," I said. "Loves control. Likeable, mind you. But listen, everything is going to be OK. Just tell her not to mess around too long and just do the C-Section."

✦

Jessica called five days later. Yes they had waited and waited and tried to turn him again. No, he had not turned. Yes, the C-Section went well. Dylan was very happy nursing and seemed "very laid back" and calm as could be.

As I checked in on him briefly at Spirit level, he was giving me the thumbs up and smiling. I wonder what he will create in his later life. He seems perfectly in control of things right now.

✦

Was She the Child of Another Man?

From my early childhood days I remember the only son of a lovely couple dying of a congenital heart defect. To fill the hole in their hearts this couple, Mary and John, adopted two sisters from a family that had been broken by divorce. The mother of that family had left not long after the birth of her fourth child. The father could not cope alone, and the family had been broken up and sent to different homes.

By the time I met Jane, the youngest of the children, she was eleven and had been in and out of foster homes. I was much the same age, so my parents suggested we spend time together and get to know each other. Jane was a thin girl, fragile, pretty and very shy. Her older sister at fifteen was already an aggressive handful and very difficult for the new adoptive parents to deal with. In those days I was too young to know much about truly helping or counseling my new friend, but we played together, which brought her out of her shell. We eventually ended up in different schools and with curriculums that took us in different directions.

Jane's sister did not stay long at her new adoptive parents' house. She was often getting into trouble with police because of drugs and alcohol. She ran away. Jane was very lonely and cut off. Though we met when we could, she felt very isolated. The worst burden she bore was that her sister, just before leaving, said Jane was the child of another man. She blamed Jane for the break-up of the family, for it was just after her birth that their real mother had left. Jane could neither prove nor disprove this statement, and it wore her down inside. She did not know her mother and barely knew her father, if indeed he was her father.

✦

Jane kept three small black and white photographs of her parents with her sisters and brothers. This was all she had of her family now. They

132

were scattered across the country, and she was the one being blamed for this family crisis. The fourth photograph was the only one of Jane. It was taken when she was a tiny baby only a few weeks old in her mother's arms. Her mother was standing beside the man Jane had, until recently, called her father. The picture was taken a few days before her mother left. As she showed me these pictures, I sensed they were her only real treasures. Shabby and torn at the edges, these photographs were her only link to whatever the truth was. Did she hope that I would have an answer to pull her out of the dark spell her sister had cast on her before leaving? Her eyes searched across the blurriness of the two-by-three inch print of herself, as if staring longer at the photograph would give her clues to her own beginning. What was she to believe? Was it her fault?

I could not begin to fathom the depths of despair she must have been feeling. I think at the time she was numb to it all. She did not cry. She sat holding the pictures, not knowing what to believe. We sat in silence together on her bed. I did not know what to say so I put my arm around her to reassure her. She was wooden, gone for a moment into her own void, a place I could not reach. So we sat quietly until her new parents called us down for tea.

Here in this big beautiful house Jane and I sat on the overstuffed couch together with an array of hot buttered scones and teacakes in front of us on the tea trolley. Mary busied herself pouring hot tea into posh china cups, while John leaned back smiling at us, smoking his pipe. We made polite conversation as we opened the fancy napkins on our knees, pretending that all was well, far removed from the reality that Jane was trying to understand. Mary and John had tried to give her so much to make up for all the sadness in her life. She felt she deserved none of it. All the finery. All the clothes and gifts. Even all the love they gave her, which was great, I knew, because they had given me the same kind of generous love when I would visit. None of it could fill the hole in her Being. She seemed at that moment like a wounded sparrow without a voice in a gilded cage meant for a songbird.

✦

By the time I went to Art College at age sixteen, Jane and I barely saw each other. Our paths were going in different directions. My father had recently died, and my own life was beginning to turn upside down. Jane had already become involved in self-destructive behaviors, such as drinking, taking drugs and hanging out with bad company. She eventually tried to commit suicide. She did not succeed and through therapy was pulled out of it.

✦

We met sometime later. She showed me burn marks on her hands where she had deliberately used matches to burn herself in disfiguring tattoos, not with flame, but with the raw phosphorous match heads twisted deep into her flesh that were later filled with blue fountain pen ink. This was before her suicide attempt and was part of some gang initiation. The deep scars on her wrists from the suicide attempts were still healing and showed up as ragged cuts from the broken glass she had used.

Luckily, Jane had been turned around with the help of the Salvation Army, who let her stay with them as she recovered. They had given her some solace as well as some direction. She no longer wanted to stay with Mary and John, though. They had asked her to return, but she felt she had let them down and refused to put them through any more of her pain.

I was glad to see that Jane was determined to make a new start of things. She was no longer drinking and was out of the drug scene. She was talking about becoming a nurse. I encouraged her to go ahead with this, as it would give her a real purpose in life.

✦

Three years later, in her last year of training and just before she would have graduated, Jane's bones began to spontaneously fracture when she would try to lift patients. This was a terrible blow to her. She suffered a great deal of pain and had to give up nursing. The last thing I heard was that she had decided to become a nun, as her grief was so great. She cut all contact with her adoptive family and friends.

✦

Her story is similar to many I have since heard and counseled. The feeling of loss never leaves a child until questions are answered and healing is done. A child needs to know the truth.

✦

An Adopted Child's Upset
at her Birth Mother
Causes Cancer in Later Life

*Traumas in early childhood or in the womb can affect a
person for a lifetime, often creating devastating illnesses.
In the case of adoption, what can bring children relief,
even as adults, is to know why they were given up.*

✦

My client Joanne tearfully asked me, "Why did Mother
give me up for adoption? Was it her choice, or did my
father force it on her?"

Joanne's birth mother was still alive and they knew each other, but
were not on happy terms.

By contacting the Higher Self of Joanne's mother at long distance on
the inner plane, I found the reason for the adoption was that she had fallen
into deep depression after the death of someone close to her. Her health
had begun to fail because she had not let the person who died go into the
Light. She was still holding on to the deceased Soul.

✦

Joanne knew that her mother had indeed fallen into deep depression
after the miscarriage of her second child and the sudden death of her own
mother in the same year. That was the same year Joanne was given up for
adoption, when she was two years old.

135

Joanne's mother had become unstable with the use of anti-depressant drugs given to her by doctors and had subsequently become an alcoholic. She was unable to care for herself or for Joanne, so Joanne was adopted by her aunt.

At Higher Self level I was able to confirm that her mother had willingly given up Joanne because she herself was too ill, and she knew her sister-in-law could handle things better. It was done out of love for Joanne and not out of hate. Joanne's father (with whom Joanne had good relations) had not coerced her into giving up Joanne. They had done what they had thought was best for her at the time.

As an adult and a nurse, Joanne could understand what losing a child and a parent could do to a woman. We were able to do the necessary closures and forgiveness. The old sadness from this event in childhood proved to be the key to the cancer that Joanne was now dealing with.

Compassion in all cases is essential. As children we may not understand our parents' dilemmas as they struggle with their own issues. In Joanne's case, her adopted mother was actually an old Soul who had traveled with her for many incarnations. It was a wonderful match for which she was grateful. Joanne had just never understood why her birth mother had apparently rejected her. This had made her feel unwanted and not good enough to be on the Earth. She felt she had done something wrong. Her Inner Child was stuck at age two and was in terrible grief and sadness about it. These negative thoughts, along with the anger of rejection, had been eating at her since then and had depleted her liver seriously, causing the onset of the cancer.

Releasing the upset Joanne had towards her mother brought a great deal of Light and healing back to her.

How the Death of an Unknown Birth Parent Affects the Adopted Child

When a child is abandoned at birth, or shortly thereafter, it has a tremendously damaging effect on the Soul. If this happens, the child may likely have no solid feelings of security or of being wanted on the Earth.

In some situations children are lucky to be adopted by truly loving parents who can heal many of these wounds. Even so, I have witnessed the dark tearing at Soul level and at other levels of Being where the child and the birth parent have been separated.

What happens to an adopted child when the birth parent dies? Especially when there has been no contact since birth and there is no knowledge of the parent's death, as the child did not know who the parent was.

I have seen two cases where the birth parent has died, unbeknownst to the child, and the child has suddenly fallen into a deep depression or feels blocked by a heavy weight. In both cases, the birth parent felt a need to know how the child survived and was dealing with guilt and grief associated with giving the child up for adoption. The parent needed closure and could not get into the Light until this was done. When there was closure, the clients in both cases felt a complete change in their energy and were at peace. The Soul of each birth parent in question was then free to go into the Light.

Many children who are adopted are not fully released by the birth parents at the emotional level. I can often see this as a cocoon that envelops the child. All the unfinished business is in this cocoon. When a woman does not want to give up her child, her hurt and grief cloaks the child. These children are often not able to be grounded as a result of this and have a difficult time with relationships. The cocoon cuts them off from the Earth, and they may often be clumsy or walk as if they are not fully present.

✦

This cocoon needs to be removed with healing work. Both the parents and the child need their energy back whole, as all suffer until this healing work is done. The "Forgiveness Prayer," can be used to help heal these wounds. See PART IV "Prayers of Forgiveness and Transition" for the transcript.

✦

The Grief of a Mother Living in Fear of Being Found by the Son She Gave up for Adoption

In my early twenties, before I met the Mayan healers who taught me in Mexico, I roomed briefly with a woman from Holland who was living at the time in Mexico City. She was a brilliant weaver and the creator of multiple-colored textured tapestries. Banks and large firms frequently bought her works for wall displays.

A large handloom stood in the middle of her apartment. Piles of yarn spilled out of big baskets by the loom. Colorful paintings and cloth were everywhere. She often took her work to New York to sell, but she lived in Mexico City most of the year.

For all of this color and creativity she was not happy, and she was drinking heavily. She was living in fear that one day the child she had given up for adoption would come looking for her. He had just turned eighteen.

✦

At the time of his birth she had been a young student living in New York, having just arrived from Holland with a strict Catholic upbringing. She explained that she became pregnant as an "innocent virgin," not knowing much about the facts of life. She had no money to raise a child and ended up staying in a church hostel with a lot of other pregnant young women. It was not a pleasant stay. All of the girls were treated like tramps and were put on early curfew. The housemother was very strict. She dared not write home to tell her parents or ask for help. As soon as the baby was born, he was taken from her. She was not allowed to hold him or to see

139

him. She was only told that he was a boy. She remembered signing some release papers.

> "I was so distraught," she said. "I couldn't even remember if the father was black or white! I had only been with two guys. Sex only twice in my life! Two different guys! I didn't know what was going on! What a bloody awful thing for that child to see on his papers, under father's name: 'unknown' . . . race: 'white, maybe black'!" she groaned and drank more wine.
>
> "God, that kid must hate me!"

They only allowed pregnant women to stay at the hostel, so immediately after the birth she was ushered along with her bags on to the street. She was on her own again. The child was taken for adoption.

Her grief and fear were obvious eighteen years later as she downed more wine while telling me her story. She drank heavily and became more and more morose. Her fear was how she would deal with her child's anger if he should ever find her. Her grief was that she would never know him. Her heavy emotional energy was certainly affecting her child at long distance, wherever he was. Both needed to be at peace.

> *So often alcohol or drugs are used in an attempt to numb the loss and grief of a situation, but they only compound the problem. It is far better to lift your Spirit through corrective prayer and healing work. As you lift your Spirit in prayer, those around you are lifted also, including any child you may have given up for adoption. Forgiveness is the key. Forgiveness of self and others, so the wounds at all levels can be healed for all parties involved.*

When the DNA Does Not Match, a Child Needs Truth

Occasionally in my work I come across a client who either has given up a child for adoption or who has been an adopted child. Other times I have had clients whose DNA does not match that of their parents, but no one has ever told them the truth.

✦

Not knowing the true birth parent can be devastating to a child. In the case of adoption, if the child has been made aware of the adoption, the child may always wonder why he or she was abandoned by the birth parents. However, not being told that he or she was adopted can lead to greater distress later in life.

✦

Children are very sensitive to unspoken truths and feel undermined, not knowing why at a conscious level. Their whole Being knows there is a lie. It can lead to a deep lack of trust in all things and a belief that the world is conspiring against them. Hushed conversations in families, innuendos, and things said behind closed doors build like a compounding conspiracy. Children pick up on the air of deceit and worry but have no way of finding the answers to their unspoken fears that something is wrong with them. They know they are different, marked in some way. The child still resonates with the DNA markers of his or her birth parents. All of the thoughts of the birth parents have a big effect on the gestating child and continue to impact the person for life.

141

I believe the truth is always best, that it is less cruel for children to know the truth than to leave them fearful of the unknown.

In the cases of two different clients, when I tracked the DNA of their fathers using the father's place of birth, date of birth and full given names at birth, the names did not match the client's own genetic codes. The DNA match was not there.

The first time this happened, I was perplexed, and strongly questioned my own Guides. However, in both cases the evidence came out later that the mothers of these two clients had most likely been with another man at the time of conception. In both cases the true father's identity was hidden in order to keep the marriage together.

✦

Why would an incoming child choose this dilemma? Perhaps the DNA of the birth father was required for some very specific reason? Perhaps it was a necessary life experience with the perceived father that otherwise could not be had? Certainly in the case of one of these clients, Charles, it had led to a very brutal upbringing, which included regular beatings by his non-blood related father.

Subconsciously we know when our spouse has been unfaithful even though we may not have physical proof. The father in this family was cruel to his "son" by another man, though his wife may never have told him the truth. Much damage had to be cleared for Charles as a result of this situation. Yet, it was his birth father's Celtic genetics that had helped bring him his knowledge of ancient healing and his innate understanding of old Celtic wisdom.

Both of Charles' parents were deceased when we began our session, as was his true birth father. Though Charles had picked up mannerisms from his non-blood father, he looked much more like the father he had never known, who was working with us on the inner plane.

I got much of the story pieced together with the Spirits of Charles' mother and his birth father. Initially, Charles was stunned and could not believe what I was saying to him.

Later when Charles called his sister, she said that he looked so much like his father she could not believe it was true, but then she remembered that their mother used to go for long walks in the park with another man while pushing Charles in the baby carriage. That man never came to the house. She said it was known that Charles's mother had had an affair with someone around the time that Charles was conceived.

> The asthma, from which Charles suffered, had come from the brutal repression by his non-blood father. It hung on his chest like a dark weight. His non-blood father's anger and rejection was immense. Now that Charles understood the background of the violence, he could begin to forgive. We lifted the weight from him and took the mother and father he had known into the Light. His birth father remained with him as a Guide once all of the forgiveness work was done. Charles himself is a brilliant healer and we have helped each other often throughout the years.

✦

The Spiritual connection between birth parents and child is strong whether they remain as a family group or not. The DNA imprint is a key to both the cellular and ancestral memories of the donor parents. I have to wonder how children born from sperm and egg bank donors relate to the world. Even though they may be grown in the host mother's womb and receive her biochemical, emotional and Spiritual influences, the basic DNA is different if it is not her own egg or her husband's sperm. How many men have given this a second thought when they donate sperm? Or women when they donate eggs?

I have not yet had the opportunity to work with a client from such a mix, but I wonder how these children adjust to the idea that they were created in such a dispassionate way? What is the imprint around them?

✦

We have Soul memory from our own lifetimes and genetic memory from our parents through which we can contact the Souls of our ancestors, as all have encoded a part of their life experience onto our DNA memory. We are also affected by our environment and human interactions as we grow.

> *I believe that in those people who work for the uplifting of humanity, the DNA takes a Spiritual charge and changes accordingly for the better. Those who work to the detriment of humanity mark their DNA with a downward*

143

retrograde frequency of negativity. Hence, the DNA codes from our birth parents carry hereditary imprints that affect the incoming Soul greatly. Not knowing who is the true genetic father or mother leaves a child without a family history trail to reference for health or Spiritual research. A yearning for truth and completion prevails.

Deep down the Soul craves for answers.

✦

PART III.

HEALING THE WOUNDS

The Many Wounds of Childhood

The idea that a child can be emotionally harmed while in the womb is perhaps a new concept for many people. Every time I meet a client it becomes obvious to me how powerfully he or she was affected in the womb, either positively or negatively, by the thoughts of the mother, the father or others.

✦

A child does not have to die physically to be effectively murdered at Soul level by his parents, by family members or by society. Neither does this have to happen in the womb. I have seen adults whose inner Spirit or "Inner Child" has been totally crushed by their parents, by actions of other family members, by overbearing societal groups or by other individuals. It can happen at any time as a child develops.

When I speak of the Inner Child, I consider this to be that fragile newly-forming aspect of the incarnating Spirit, the individualized Spirit coming from the Source, which includes a composite of all the levels of consciousness needed for this physical existence. The Inner Child is in a sensitive, formative state as it over-lights the growth of the fetus during gestation. Thoughts and feelings have a great effect at this early stage of growth. It is a fragile time. The thoughts, feelings and events around a pregnant woman leave a deep imprint on the cell growth and mental, emotional and physical function of the fetus. What the mother eats or drinks, as well as any kind of sickness she suffers, also has an enormous effect on the development of a child.

✦

147

A child that is loved and wanted has feelings of security and love deeply embedded in his or her Being. Each cell gets programmed in a positive way for health and strength. What happens in these early stages forms the ground-spring from which he or she will go forward in life.

The Inner Child has a direct link to the Source when it begins its journey into the physical world and knows the mission for which it is intended in this lifetime. When I meet a client for the first time, I look for the Inner Child. If I find a happy Inner Child, it tells me that the client is on track with her mission and that her Spiritual flow is intact. When the Inner Child is joyful and full of enthusiasm for life, it permeates all the aspects of that person's Being. These people are usually radiant, looking and acting as if they have eternal youth. In a way they do. The Inner Child is at home with its own Spiritual Source from which it is completely nurtured.

✦

The clients who come to me, shaky in their belief that they have a right to be on this Earth, have low self esteem, numerous illnesses of origins their doctors cannot find, who are inclined towards suicide or have no energy to live, are classic examples of people who have a wounded Inner Child and may not have been wanted in the womb.

The wounded Inner Child becomes splintered off from its Source because of some great disruption in its life path at some point in time since the moment of conception.

If I find the client was indeed wanted as a child, perhaps then some violence or abuse has occurred since birth, or some kind of severe handicap, caused by a nutritional, medical or drug problem, has caused them to be impaired. There may be many other reasons, such as surgeries that went wrong, damage from a forceps delivery, or infections in the womb. The list is endless.

Whatever the cause, the Inner Child will often shut down and throw a defense system around itself, enabling it to control, from its own dark and hidden place, all the events in the client's lifetime from a contorted and painful worldview. Often the client has no idea why she reacts to certain situations the way she does. The Inner Child is silently in control far from conscious memory.

When the Inner Child loses its way and is cut off from its Source, no amount of drugs or operations can fix that person. The Inner Child needs its wounds healed in order to be reintegrated into wholeness with its Source and welcomed back into the heart and Soul. If this is not done, that person may become listless, seriously ill, or even suicidal as the Inner Child continues to suffer or tries to leave.

✦

Most clients will rarely remember what happened in the womb, but often they will know if their parents wanted them or not, or if they had been planned, or if they were an "accident."

If a mother considers abortion, but then changes her mind, she has still imprinted the child with fear for its life and a feeling of lack of worth in this world. I can see the thoughts of abortion from a mother imprinted on a child after it is born. Nothing ever seems to make up for that first breach of trust. The child will always be seeking approval from the parent, will always be needy, and will never feel like there is enough love or security. Why? It is because the Inner Child was partially cut off from its Source by negative thoughts at a time when it could not defend itself and when its only security was the womb of the mother. The imprint then becomes one of not being wanted, rather than one of love. Is it any wonder that these children struggle throughout their whole lives looking for someone to love them enough? But the hole that needs to be filled cannot be filled from the outside. It is a wound that leaks life force from deep within the Spiritual aspect of the Inner Child. The wound usually shows at the Higher Self level as a dark split, where the Spirit's link to the Source is partially severed. This wound in the Higher Self is similar to the imprint that may be found after a near-death experience or attempted suicide. Life force is lost as it flows into the Spiritual chalice of the body at the most precious level. This is where the damage must be found and healed. The Inner Child needs to be reconnected to the Divine Source and know that it is loved. It needs to be nurtured and loved, then returned healed in Spirit to the heart center of the body, where it belongs.

Many adopted children I have met do not appear to have their feet on the ground. They seem to be cut off from the Earth by their birth parents, whom they may never have seen but who still have a tremendous effect on them at long distance. The grief or rage of a mother who gave up a child can have long and profound effects on the child. Her emotional bonds can cocoon or suffocate the child on the inner plane and can cut the child off from ever being able to truly be in the world and know his own feelings. If the mother fears being found by her child, she may put up barriers on the emotional plane that will haunt the child forever with a feeling of being always unwanted. Such barriers will block the child from life and love. The same is true for a father who wants no part of a child's life. His indifference or anger will have similar repercussions.

An unexpected child who caused parents to "have to get married" often bears the same imprint of not being wanted, especially if there was no real love in the marriage. Sadly, they may become the "reason" and focus for everything that is wrong with their parents' lives.

A child who loses her parents to death or divorce will often have feelings of rage, upset and unworthiness, believing at some deep level she caused the problem and has been abandoned because of it. Often in an attempt to protect the child, the Spirit of the parent has cocooned her in such a way that the child cannot progress, causing the child to fall into deep depression or even become suicidal as the parent's own grief and loss affects them.

Many times the last child born to older parents is unexpected. I have seen many who suffer the feelings of not being wanted in this situation, especially if there is a large age gap between them and the other siblings. They often feel left out and are seeking attention and recognition any way they can get it, often through excessive behavior.

All these are issues to be cleared through healing work, which takes time and dedication. A person must want to be healed and be ready to forgive past hurts in order to move beyond the crippling of past traumas. For the unwanted child, or the child that feels unloved or abandoned, the answer is to get back in touch with his or her own Source through Spiritual healing. Reaching back to the true oneness of Spirit and love at the highest level brings the life force back to the body.

✦

I can usually figure out when the first big event occurred in a client's life that cut her off from her Source by the apparent age of the Inner Child. The Inner Child will be stuck in that time frame and not have grown in stature with the physical person. It is as if this part has been left behind, while the rest moved on with a feeling of numbness and loss. Sometimes this has happened before birth and sometimes in very early childhood, but I am immediately able to see the details when I ask the Angels to show me the Inner Child.

I see the Inner Child in the same way I see Spirit. I can converse with it and find out what happened. Often the Inner Child is more lucid about events than the client who is with me.

I have found the Inner Child escaping in an imaginary hot air balloon rather than facing reality, or hiding in a coal bunker to avoid punishment, or deep underground in a black ball of rage after being beaten, or locked in a dark prison cell. These images are sometimes symbolic, or sometimes a reality from early life. However, when I ask Christ and the Angels to bring Light and healing to the Inner Child, the truth comes out. The real scene begins to be revealed that caused the Inner Child to hide.

Events that are painful become deeply hidden in the subconscious, but the Inner Child who has witnessed these things remembers, and when it remembers, the memories flash back into reality for my clients. They will often say, "Yes I remember that now. How could I have ever forgotten it?" Out will come a traumatic event in all its detail. That is when the healing work can begin. As forgiveness is done, energy that was left behind is healed and reintegrated.

✦

The key here is to remember that we must go beyond the trauma and take our Spiritual life force back into our own keeping. Bearing a grudge or anger towards a person who hurt us only depletes our Being. The intent must be to heal and not to blame nor wallow in past hurts as an excuse for how we are now. By forgiving and going beyond the damage that was done, we unlock the door to our own Spiritual flow again. We must nurture our Inner Child, who is the keeper of our Sacred mission on Earth. In the end we are the only ones who can heal ourselves. Others may guide us, but ultimately we are the creators of our own life path by the choices we make each day. We can choose to love or to hate. These simple decisions change our lives dramatically, for better or worse.

✦

We all have wounds in one form or another. Every one of us carries a global inheritance of wars and violence and grief. We mirror our parents' actions just as they mirrored their parents', for their influences are embedded deeply at our core level. In order to heal this planet, we first need to heal ourselves and to remember where we came from. Not one of us is truly whole. We all have work to do. Thousands suffer silently, not knowing who they are or why they feel cut off from themselves.

Be brave enough to ask for the healing Light to help you and remember the true glory of who you are.

✦

The Lost Legions on the Inner Plane

My main focus for this book has been the unborn children and those who died at birth or shortly thereafter without healing and rites of transition. It is to these forgotten children I am now giving a voice. The cries I hear on the inner plane from these children are overwhelming. I believe that something needs to be done on a global scale to bring these children into the Light and bring them peace. We are at a crisis point around the globe.

Why should I refer to it as a crisis? Apart from the obvious suffering of the millions of children who have died, the entire fabric of humanity is shifting as a result of the damage that has been done to the Souls of these children. Women suffer, men suffer and families suffer. A great weight lies upon the shoulders of each individual on this planet on the inner plane, but because it is unseen on the physical realm, and the discomfort it brings is misunderstood, most people turn to drugs, alcohol, overeating or another form of behavior in order to dull their senses to the reality of what is really happening. In large part, I find people are allowing themselves to be Spiritually unconscious. They are being dictated to by television and mass media. It is as if they have forgotten what it is to feel for themselves and how to act as the independent Spirits that they really are. Spiritual Consciousness is being lulled asleep. Masses of people are out of touch with their Inner Spirit. Perhaps it is too painful for them to awaken, for then they must witness the Truth and act accordingly.

I believe we are facing an ever-increasing weight of darkness as more and more atrocities happen around the world. Whether it is through war, in prisons, in schools or between parents and children, the violence continues. I also believe the desperation of Souls trapped between the worlds drives many in the Physical Body into depression, mental and physical illness, suicide and even wars. As a global society we become more and more unbalanced the further we travel from our Sacred connection to God.

I do not think there is one of us that is not greatly affected by the untimely deaths of others. It is my belief and my experience that our deeper knowing feels the rage and bitterness that is cried out from these lost Souls as they reach out for help, but all too often we close our eyes and ears.

✦

Many of these Souls had a life plan and an important mission on Earth equally as great as any you or I believe we have now. These Souls may have become some of our greatest teachers, artists, musicians, mathematicians and scientists and have brought in wisdom far more beautiful than anything we now know. I have seen many Souls who have been trapped and damaged through abortion become radiant and magnificent Beings of Light once we have done the healing work for them.

Other wounded Souls of children are often just limping blindly from one difficult life cycle to the next with no life plan at all, with large parts of their being trapped in many other lives. In desperation, they may have torn free from the grip of one life trauma and its people and events, but doing so has fractured the Soul. They may never fully reach the Light between lifetimes as a result. They are endlessly drawn on by unfinished business from one catastrophe to another. Theirs is a sad fate, unless they can be found and helped with the healing work.

These Souls, who are reborn without ever reaching the Light for true healing and rejuvenation, often do not remember their connection to God. They have wandered between the worlds in a pitiful condition and then they come back into the birth cycle with huge scars from their previous lives. Their tendency is to return to similar situations, often with the very same people they fought against, as this is where they are pulled to by their unfinished karmic ties. These same patterns may repeat for many birth cycles until the Soul has learned its lessons and lets go of the negative emotions that have bound it. It is the entangled energy links between people that draw them back together for completion. When forgiveness is done, the binding negativity can be released. Then Souls will have their own energy returned, and they can be free.

✦

I witness the pain of these lost Souls every day in my work, as clients arrive with their various illnesses. Clients come to me tired and in pain, weeping or just exhausted, not knowing why they feel such pain, or why they are suicidal, or facing cancer, or some other grave disease. As we take the Souls of these children and other Souls who may be trapped in the energy field of the client into the Light, the pain of the client also lifts and Light returns to their Being. Yet, for every child's Soul I take into the Light, I know that many more will die each day without help. Many more parents and families will feel the ongoing pain for years to come. This is what saddens me and why I must write this book.

✦

For every child who dies without a voice and a rite of transition into the Light, many more children suffer in the physical realm because they are as sensitive to the Soul's pain as I am. Children are usually much more open to the Spiritual realms than their parents. Children often know the Spirit of the incoming child and are communicating with him or her even before birth. It causes the living child great distress to know a sibling has died, for any reason, but more particularly if the child believes the death was a deliberate choice.

Over the years I have learned to use my seeing and hearing on the inner planes safely, but when I was a child, some of the things I saw and heard scared me. Children do not have the ability to switch off or tune out the very real crying Spirits around them. It can affect them deeply in their dreams as well as in their waking life as a continual heaviness and fear.

✦

Abortion is a sad situation for all concerned. I have compassion for all involved because I have been there. I know it is a decision made in desperate circumstances. I also know there are very real financial concerns around having a child, as well as health questions if a mother's life is in danger. A child must be wanted in order for that child to have a happy life. There are many arguments both for and against abortion. Beyond it all is a higher Truth that I believe we must all someday be aware of, that

155

the Spirit of the child is connected to the embryo even in the early days of gestation.[1]

If the connection between the Spirit and the Physical Body is severed, the Physical Body will die. If there is violence or negative emotion during the moment of death, then the Soul can become entrapped and not be able to reach the Light, or it may only partially reach the Light, leaving a part of itself locked in time with whatever, or whomever, was holding it back.

The Spirit is an aspect of God. Through the Spirit we have our connection to that Divine Source. The Spirit creates the Soul in its own likeness, but at a frequency slightly slower and denser in order to begin the process of building the matrix of bodies that become the template for the Physical Body. The Soul can be very ancient, having lived many lifetimes, or it may be young with only a few lifetimes of experience.

Some argue that the Spirit only enters at birth. I can only say that it is my belief and my experience that the Spirit is connected at all times to the developing fetus. A premature child can still live if its body is whole, so the matter of month's gestation is not the issue. In my opinion, the question should not be "When does the Spirit fully enter the child's body?" It should be "Is the fetus in the womb a Spiritual Being?"

I would have to answer that the fetus is over-lighted by, and connected to, a Spirit at all times. Without an over-lighting Spirit the Physical Body of the fetus cannot develop. If the over-lighting Spirit is withdrawn, the fetus will die. They are aspects of the same Being. Though the Spirit exists independently as a Being in its own right before conception takes place, the Physical Body cannot exist independently of the Spirit and still live. The Physical Body of the fetus is the outward and visible expression of the Spirit even in its earliest phase of growth. From day one, each cell is interpenetrated with the multi-dimensional aspects of the new child's incoming Spirit, the influences of its parents and of the Creator. All have a part in the cosmic dance of energies that help the newly-forming levels of the body develop. In my view the fetus cannot be thought of as just a group of inanimate cells. It is a living Being over-lighted by the consciousness

---

[1] *For those who have had an abortion and may be reading this information for the first time, please do not despair. The prayers in the back of this book will help you and your child's Soul heal, and can assist your child's Soul return to the Light at this difficult time.*

of Spirit. They exist together as a unit. The fetus has a consciousness at all times; therefore, it is as much a Spiritual Being as you or I.

One could say the Spirit is in a Holy Communion with the flesh of the body of the fetus as it grows. As such, we should address the child's Spirit with as much respect as we would any other Spiritual Being.

Our Spirit is always connected to the Source. For most of us it descends only partially even at birth because our small bodies could not handle such Light and dynamic energy. Sometimes a Spirit may only bring a small percentage of itself into incarnation, choosing to keep the larger part in the Spiritual realms. Many of us are walking around barely present on the Earth as conscious Spiritual Beings. It is as though we are sleepwalkers on the Earth, unaware of our vast Spiritual potential, involved only in our material wants and physical desires. However, we can awaken, if we so choose, and bring our full Spiritual Presence to Earth. Spiritual Masters are able to bring their Divine Spiritual Aspects fully into their bodies. Great Light flows through them, and their immense presence is felt and seen by their followers.

It is important for all Souls to be free to bring their Spiritual Presence to Earth in full and not be trapped in a difficult death process. The entrapment between the worlds of the Souls of children who have died without proper rites of transition is a very sad situation for which we are all now paying. We all bear the burden of these lost Souls, because they are a part of the greater Spiritual Consciousness of Humanity of which we are all a part.

Some clients have asked why God did not take care of this Himself. My answer is that we are all given free will. If we choose to hold on to a Soul because of grief, shame or anger, we have made it difficult for that Soul to rise freely from our Being. It is our choice to hold on, or to let go.

The Spirit of a child is eternal, as are the Spirits of us all. I believe we are born and reborn many times. This is how we have chosen to evolve. We need to learn to speak to the Spirit of the child and find out what our agreements are, just as the aborigines of Australia, or the women of India do. If it is not yet an appropriate time for birth, it can be discussed gently with the incoming Spirit. In the first few weeks, even though the embryo may not yet be viable for living outside of the womb, it is the developing living expression of a conscious Spiritual Being. The Spirit is connected to the embryo by a golden cord of Light. It can hear our thoughts and respond to them at a Spiritual level. From what I witnessed with my own child, if the Spirit chooses to leave and break that connection, then the over-lighting Spiritual life force is gone, and a natural miscarriage will occur.

✦

Many women who are sensitive know the instant they are pregnant. They feel the child's Spirit connect to them as a warm rush of joyful energy. Many have seen their child's Spirit in dreams weeks or days ahead and know they will become pregnant.

As a pregnancy progresses, the Spirit of the child becomes more deeply connected with the fetus. At first it would seem the child is in a dream state and can talk with its Guides and Teachers on the higher Spiritual realms, if it has maintained that contact. (Damaged Souls may not have this conscious contact.) The child's Spirit comes and goes between the higher realms and the small body being formed, but always it is connected by the golden cord of Light. As the months continue to pass, and the different levels of consciousness build around the fetus, the Spirit becomes more deeply enmeshed with the newly-forming body. Gradually, enough energy is built to enable the Soul to become consciously aware of itself in its new body.

It is important to remember that everything the mother is exposed to during that time affects the child's Soul. Not only food and drink should be pure and healthful, but also the emotional state of the parents, and what is around them in the environment. Violence in the household or on television imprints the mother and child. Every thought a mother has affects her blood chemistry. Uplifting thoughts create a healthy body; negative thoughts create sickness.

Stress can change the body chemistry and make it harder for a pregnancy to come to full term. I have been told that acupuncturists are trained to avoid certain key points on the energy meridians, which could shut down the energy to the womb and cause a miscarriage in a pregnant woman. Perhaps stress can also shut down these same meridians.

Many clients have told me that their miscarriage happened in the first few weeks of pregnancy when they were upset or worried about their relationship with the father of their child. They may not have been married, or the marriage was breaking down. Though they did not recall having consciously spoken to the child, the child's Spirit may have understood the situation and chosen to leave, or stress may have induced the miscarriage. If the parents have not held on to the Soul of the child, or bound it with arguments, it will have been free to go without too much trauma. Yet sadness and loss remains hidden deep within the parents until the release work is done, particularly in the woman's body.

Often these cases are simple enough, as only a little residual energy is left behind by the departing Soul, though I always check and do a clearing with the "Forgiveness Prayer" to be sure everyone has his energy back as blessed Christ Light.

✦

The sad part for me to witness is the emotional struggle of a woman who becomes pregnant with a man she loves, who subsequently leaves her because of the pregnancy. She might go from being joyful about the incoming child, to severe depression over the loss of her mate and the difficulties of rearing a child alone. The further the pregnancy has progressed, the harder it is for a child's Soul to leave, as its life forces are now deeply involved with the creation of the new body. Its Being is now involved with the energies of both parents and their genetic codes and karma. The turmoil in the mother can cause a tremendous tangling of energy as the mother struggles with the choices between abortion, adoption or keeping the child. The child's Soul becomes enmeshed and cannot leave if an abortion takes place or a miscarriage or stillbirth occurs. If no abortion or miscarriage takes place, and the child's Spirit is determined enough to weather the emotional storms and come to full term, the struggle will show deeply in that child's psyche throughout adulthood.

I feel that many Souls stay strongly implanted in the womb for karmic reasons and go through unimaginable traumas because they do not want to give up their right to birth. Sometimes it may be their only chance to complete karma with one or the other parent. In such a case, if their chance is cut short, they may become enraged. Illness will likely occur in the mother and possibly the father (depending upon whom the major karmic link was with), as the battle never ends until forgiveness is done and the child's Soul is released.

I have heard some say that Souls choose to have the experience of being aborted. I personally cannot believe that so many have chosen abortion as a life path. From what I have seen, it is not the case. No child's Soul I have worked with has ever said, "This is perfect, just what I planned." Most are terrified and very upset. Their wounds are great.

Others ask, "Then, if the Spirit can see so much ahead of time, why did it choose to come in to a situation where it was not wanted? Why did its Teachers and Angels not warn it ahead of time?" To which I answer, we are given free will. A woman or her mate may suddenly change their minds once the child has committed itself to the life process. Or an incoming Soul may be a wounded Soul that has lost touch with the Angels and is barely conscious of its own Spirituality and can no longer hear its Spiritual advisors. The Soul may have just recently passed on and has never reached the Light to review the options available to it. It may even have been previously entrapped by its parents and never have left their energy fields, and this is the only way for a possible release. The karmic ties that have bound it previously may pull so hard that this child is compelled to be born to these parents. It seeks to return to gather up the life force that belongs to it that was enmeshed perhaps lifetimes ago.

✦

Many people reincarnate with chunks of their Souls missing from past lives. This can be the reason for their health problems. They are the lucky ones who were able to pull enough of their energy out over time to continue their evolutionary path. Other Souls can stay trapped, cut off from their Spiritual Source, and exist in a level of darkened unawareness often reliving their last moments over and over with those they struggled with. This is what some call hell. Some people, even now in their own physical lives, are living in a darkened hell of unconsciousness and have no idea that there is a Spiritual world around them. They are ignorant of what beauty could be theirs because their focus is one of greed, hate or some other negative emotion.

A Soul that comes into a new body while parents are using drugs or alcohol or abusing each other will most likely be a damaged Soul returning to a level of energy similar to what he or she has previously known. It would be rare for a high level Spiritual Being to consciously choose to enter into a birth situation fully aware of severe damage that will likely occur. Parents who are Spiritually aware and praying for a child of great Spirituality, while purifying and preparing themselves, will draw an advanced Soul into their family. However, as Spiritual Beings we have free will. I have one client who chose to come into a very harsh wartime

160

situation to protect her mother, with whom she had a strong Spiritual past life connection. It was her desire to stop more difficult energies from entering her mother's womb, which may have been attracted in that wartime situation. This client came in with the desire to bring peace to both sides.

✦

Today few churches really understand the rites of transition for the Soul. Words are spoken in haste without the full conscious request from the higher realms for help in the transition. People are left with their grief without fully understanding how to let go, and so their unfinished emotional issues bind the Soul of the deceased to them. Instead of understanding it is necessary to release that Soul back to the Light, they hold on. The Soul might in the end tear herself away with such force that a part of the griever goes too, or the departing Soul may leave a part of his or her own energy behind. Either way, this is not a healthy situation and leaves damage for both parties.

With older married couples often one will die soon after the other, as their ties are so strong. This does not have to be a negative situation if love is the true link between them. Sustained grief usually comes when there is unfinished business between a deceased Soul and the person left behind. The desire to say they are sorry and to forgive is their greatest need. It is the healing balm that ultimately lets them release each other.

> One client in her thirties came to me with a huge, dark field attached to her Higher Self that pulled a large part of her life force away from this life into another. The energy attached was screaming, "I will not let you go!" When I traced it back to her previous life, I found her as an elderly lady dying in an antebellum home in one of the Southern states of the USA about a hundred years ago. Her husband was grief stricken about her leaving and had held onto her Spirit all these years. We did the forgiveness and release work. As her Higher Self finally became whole, her strength was returned. Her husband's energy was returned to him as Christ Light.

✦

161

Some people have had near-death experiences, and have gone into the Light but have been able to return to their bodies because the connection between the Higher Self and the Physical Body has not been severed completely. I can tell if someone has had a critical life and death experience because the cut or gash mark still shows at Higher Self as it connects to the Soul, but there will still be life force flowing, if only partially, through the remaining connection. It is like looking at a cord of Light partly cut through. The Spirit can travel long distances from the Physical Body and Soul if it wishes and still return, as long as the golden cord of Light between them remains intact.

Sometimes people are brought to me after attempting suicide because they could not let the Soul go that was trying to leave. The Soul's pull to the Light made the griever believe suicide was the only way out of the great sadness they felt. Once the clearing work is done, however, and both parties have their rightful energy back, joy can return to life. The departing Soul can finally be healed in the Light. The client will be at peace.

Those who commit suicide rarely reach the Light without help because their moment of death is usually one of great turmoil and sadness. It can wreak havoc on the family left behind, causing great illness and other suicides to occur. Suicides take special care and gentleness to discover what the Soul needs, but they can be healed and taken into the Light. The gateways between the realms need to be closed firmly once a Soul has been taken into the Light so other family members are not pulled upon.

Over the years I have witnessed many Souls struggling to be free who have been trapped between worlds. For every war or sudden violent death, many have been left behind. In the moment of death negative emotions such as fear, grief, anger, hatred, lust, greed or vengeance can cloud the Spiritual vision. These heavy emotions create a dark veil between the Soul and its Spiritual Source. This can have a profound impact on a Soul's ability to reach the Light.

Many of these trapped Souls do not have an understanding of the Spiritual realms available to them, so they refuse to leave the Earth plane consciousness, which is all they know. Fear keeps them clinging firmly to this physical realm. Even though Angels may try to guide them, these

Souls may be in such a dark place they cannot see or hear the Angels beside them. Either they have no Spiritual belief system in life after death, or they have become too entangled in the bitter emotional trauma at the moment of death to be able to be free. A large part of them may be caught up in the emotional fields of others who may have died with them and are also trapped, or who may have been the very cause of their death. Until this tangled energy is released and forgiven, it will hold the Souls back. The Angels cannot force Souls into the Light. Every Soul has free will. Many Souls, after death in war or in unjust situations, choose to fight on firmly believing they are still alive, which of course they are in their Non-Physical Bodies. This is similar to my experience of leaving my body when I was sixteen. I was fully conscious and could see the world with my Non-Physical Body. The difference was that my Physical Body had not died; I had just momentarily slipped out of it.

These Souls who seek revenge stay trapped in the lower worlds. It is no wonder to me that places of bloodshed have a dark feeling or that wars continue sometimes for generations. Souls whose lives have been cut short through murder, war or other sudden death are often not given the last rites of transition to help them complete what needs to be forgiven. They usually have a great sadness and anger in the moment of their death when they see their life has been cut short. It is their anger and unfinished business with those who killed them, as well as the sadness of their families that binds them to this Earth plane. It is the pain of the deceased Soul that will most often cause those on the physical plane to want to avenge them.

✦

It is the Earthbound Souls seeking a voice that can cause any number of illnesses in those who have a Physical Body. The Soul's grief or anger tears at the fabric of the family left behind as well as that of the nation. Over the years I have worked with many thousands of these Souls, and I take them into the Light whenever I find them.

Often I will come across Earthbound Souls in old battlefields, but they can be anywhere that violent death has occurred, or they may be attached to family members that have not let them go. Some say what is left behind is a memory or negative thought form in these places and not the Soul. I have seen both. Places and living Beings bear a memory of events on the subtle matrix of the inner plane. These events can keep replaying if a tremendous amount of emotion was involved.

These original events have created negative thought forms that are left behind, which are tangible to most people if they have any sensitivity. Most people can tell if an argument has just taken place in a room that is now empty. Likewise, most people feel a cold heaviness in a place where there has been an unpleasant death.

✦

Therefore, there are different levels of release work to be done. There are trapped Souls, who never left the place where they died, and there are aspects of Souls left in a place and time. There may also be negative thought forms created by an individual or a group, which need clearing. Understanding exactly what to clear can be difficult at times; however, working with Christ, Mary, the Angels, and our Guides and Teachers, the work can be done.

A negative thought form is created by the Mental Body of a person holding a strong, continuous thought (perhaps a desire to kill) that is then filled with a powerful emotional force (such as hatred) from the Emotional Body. The energy of both of these bodies is life force that belongs to the creator of the thought form. If it gets left behind in a place or another person's energy field, it will deplete the original creator of the negative thought form and will also cause illness to those exposed to it.

There is a difference between an Earthbound Soul (or Entity) and a negative thought form. A negative thought form, made by an individual or group, contains mental and emotional energy that can be fairly easily dissolved with corrective prayer and Christ Light and returned to wherever it came from.

An Earthbound Soul, however, is a living Being and part of a greater Spirit that has been cut off from its memory of its Source of Light and God Consciousness. It must be treated with respect as a part of God's Divine Creation no matter how far from the Light it has fallen. God exists in even the darkest places. Nothing exists outside of God. However, Souls can forget they have a connection with God when terrible hurts have befallen them. In that forgetting they lose their way and fall into darkness.

✦

It is because these lost Souls relate more to the physical realms that we in the Physical Body can help. We can intercede on behalf of these Souls and act as intermediaries for the Higher Realms. Often I have found Souls who will readily speak to me who clearly cannot see the finer frequencies of the Angels and Spiritual Realms around them. It is even less likely they could see these realms when they had a Physical Body. After the healing Christ Light is gently brought in at a frequency they can handle, and the forgiveness and release work are done with whomever they are entangled, they are usually able to see and hear the Angels. We are then able to take them to the Light.

When a Soul is finally helped out of the darkness, it is important to take it to a level of Light that it can handle and to gently lift it to a greater understanding and place of healing. This is the same as taking a person from a cave with no light and protecting his eyes before exposing him to direct sunlight. In the same manner these Souls need time to adapt. Since they have been damaged, they need time to rebuild and reconnect to their Source, with the help of the Angels, before reincarnating elsewhere.

If a Soul has been unable to heal itself before taking on another body, the wounds from the previous life act as downward negative energy depleting the new life that is being created. These wounds usually show up as a gaping hole or wound on the Soul that leaks life force or binds it with darkness. This can create difficult health problems in the newly-forming body and only compounds the level of pain for that Soul in the new incarnation. Healing needs to be done, therefore, with prayers and forgiveness after every difficult life situation. Each one of us needs to heal ourselves. By using the "Forgiveness Prayer" it is possible to retrieve lost energy belonging to the Soul and begin the healing process.

✦

I believe there are so many millions of lost Souls that are weighing on the consciousness of the living that we are facing a massive Spiritual crisis of a dimension far greater than the holocaust. This global crisis affects everything. Our loss of Spiritual direction affects every level of humanity. It is my deepest belief that a great act of compassion must happen. A forgiveness for every person involved needs to happen, and rites of transition need to be done for all of the many wounded Souls, no matter who they may be.

This needs to be done with grace. I do not mean exorcism, where a Soul is driven away. I am talking about Sacred and healing rites through which these sad, damaged Souls can be brought back into wholeness and

165

returned to the Light in grace, where all parties are forgiven for everything that has been done.

Without forgiveness, nothing moves.

✦

What I believe must now happen is an awakening of all humanity to the great task we have ahead of clearing the vast karmic debts we have incurred globally. We must release the lost Souls of millions of children, and all other trapped Souls, and help them return to the Source, the Light of God for healing. The wounds of parents, families and nations can then begin to be healed. All people must learn to forgive and be forgiven and become reconnected to their own Sacred Source. When there are many of us committed to working compassionately with the Light of the Creator, the Heart of the World can be healed, one person at a time, nation by nation.

We are all connected. Everything any one of us thinks and does affects all humanity in more powerful ways than most can comprehend. Then let us lift our thoughts to the Light together and heal ourselves.

✦

As John Donne said:
"No man is an island entire of itself,
Each is a part of the whole a part of the main.
". . . Any man's death diminishes me. . . "

It is time for every nation to wake up to the needs of its people and, using its own form of prayer, ask that these lost Souls be taken into the Light.

Massive action in the form of prayer is now essential.

✦

166

Walk with the Angels in the Light

I believe that we have all come from One Source, and it is to that Source that we will all return. However, this return does not have to happen at death, as it is an unveiling of consciousness that we can all become aware of in our everyday lives if we choose. The Source is beyond thought and physical existence, yet It permeates all levels of our Being. This One Source is everywhere and in us at all times. Only our forgetting gives us temporary blindness to the Truth. It is our own thoughts that darken our ability to see the Light of the Source within us and around us and in all Creation.

The Source is the Spiritual matrix upon which all levels of our Being have been built. At death our individualized Spirit gathers back to itself all aspects of its Soul, leaving the Physical Body behind as a shell. When the Soul returns to its Spiritual Source, it retains all the memories from that lifetime.

Life and death are similar to breathing out and breathing in. Instead of thinking that one is a beginning and the other an ending, I think of them more as acts in an on-going drama of the unfolding Universal Consciousness, where we play out our roles by casting off old costumes and changing them for new ones in time for the next scene. It is through our various roles that we learn all levels of becoming a conscious co-creator with God. I believe that sometimes we travel as groups of Souls together, working on a specific area of the evolutionary plan. Nothing is ever static. The universe is unfolding like a lotus flower with a million petals, and within each petal is another lotus flower expanding with millions of petals, each one representing an individualized Spiritual aspect of the Creator.

✦

I do not see death, under normal circumstances, as a terrible thing, but rather as a wonderful return to the higher levels of consciousness where the heaviness of the Physical Body no longer restricts the Spirit. Yet, we do not have to die to experience this beauty. We can bring it to Earth even now through the intentional shifting of our consciousness to the higher levels. It is to those levels we must go to achieve true healing. This is when it can be helpful to have someone who is fully acquainted with these levels to help you in prayers. This person can act as a resonating field and hold the frequency of the Source, which is pure Unconditional Love. This helps bring your own Soul into the correct resonance once again. It is something akin to a tuning fork resonating when the frequency for which it is tuned is sounded.

And so it is in helping lost Souls return to the Light. Each Soul still has that aspect of the Source hidden in its Being like a small holographic chip of memory. It is awaiting the correct Light and frequency to awaken and illuminate the Truth of its origin and bring it back into the Light of Spiritual Consciousness. When the Light of Love comes in, the emotional cords that have bound the Soul in darkness and illusion are dissolved away. The healer, working with Christ, Mary and the Angels, can hold that resonance of Christ Light, the Light of Love, and it is through this beautiful resonance that the Soul's connection to its Source is reawakened. The Soul can then be brought back into alignment with its Spiritual Source and be healed.

So you see, this is not actually about going anywhere as much as it is about changing the energetic frequency of one's thoughts and feelings. Just as in tuning in to a radio station, the choice of frequency and the channel is up to you. What you focus your thoughts and feelings upon is the key to life. Focusing on hate, anger or other negative emotions will lock your mind away from the higher vibrations of love, joy and happiness.

✦

In order to move into the place of healing, you will need to choose carefully from this time on who you spend your time with and what you focus your mind upon.

We are all connected, much like the cells in the greater body of humanity. Whatever our thoughts are, they affect all things. I see this in reality as I work with my clients. I see how dark thoughts become a heavy weight upon the body and sap the cells of their strength. This is what causes many diseases and psychoses. It makes no difference whether the thoughts have been created by the person who is suffering from them, or by someone who is angry with them, the effect is the same. The damage is great and can even cause death in the long run if it is not cleared. Negative thoughts and emotions cause the life force to be suffocated.

I have also witnessed what happens with healing Light, forgiveness and prayers that allow the Soul of a person to become whole. For me, one of the most beautiful moments in a session occurs when all the work is done and the true Spirit of the client, the individualized essence of the Creator, which I call the Higher Self, becomes fully realized in the body. Radiance and beauty shine in all directions as the Higher Self is made manifest.

As I see the Light of the Creator shining from the person before me, I am made humble and I stand in awe of their Sacred beauty. For my clients and for myself this is the moment that we strive for. I call it coming home to One's Self, becoming whole and at One with God, the Source of all things. In these moments, a beautiful Light fills the room and my clients are in a state of grace, often for the first time since they began their journey in the womb. I see flashes of Light as the wings of Angels hover around them guiding the Higher Self in. Peace enters them and they feel a sense of joy they have likely never known. Their old internal war is over. Once again they are at one with God. It isn't that God ever left them, they simply had lost touch with their ability to see and feel God's presence, as their minds and hearts became heavy with their physical day-to-day problems.

They often ask me, "Will this last?" I tell them they must no longer allow dark thoughts into their Being, and, if they have bad thoughts, they must immediately cast them out and hold on to the Light. It is their duty to maintain their Spiritual connection with prayers.

It takes time to learn the skills of holding the Light. A Spiritual practice of regular prayer, forgiveness of ourselves and others, and affirmations to serve the Light are essential. These are the only ways that we will lift the world out of darkness into the next level of grace.

After going out into the world and dealing with the general hurly-burly of existence, most clients return for additional balancing, but each time it is easier for them to maintain their internal peace for a longer period of time. They learn what throws them out of balance, and they learn how to correct it. Step by step, they come closer to feeling the Love of the Creator as a continuous flow of consciousness.

✦

I have known great Teachers in my life, wonderful people who have inspired many thousands with their words, and others who have come only to help me in the still silence as I have traveled alone. I am so grateful for their presence in my life. Often a Teacher has come for only a short time and then moves on to other countries or passes between the worlds to teach from the realms of Spirit. It is with their help that I have learned what I now know, and that I continue to learn. It is these great Teachers, along with Christ and Mary and the Angels, who are now telling me that this work of healing needs to be done. The weight and burden on our families is too much, and the deaths of many innocent children are weighing on us globally.

If you could see how this weight affects all of humanity, you would understand why so many are ill, why there is so much mental anxiety and distress, why families turn against each other, and why divorce and violence happens. When you understand these things it soon becomes obvious why nations rise against nations. The darkness needs to lift.

✦

It is time for each of us to first purge our own Soul of unwanted darkness and then help in the greater work of lifting trapped Souls into the Light.

We can all walk in the Light with the Angels while we are still in a Physical Body on the Earth. For our health and the health of our loved ones, it is time now to let go of those who have passed on that we have been clinging to. When we hold onto them, our grief binds and hurts them, and we prevent them from making their transition into the Light.

It is important to understand that grief beyond a short time becomes a powerful binding cord around those we have lost. They then struggle to be free. In that struggle we feel even more pain, and so do they. We must let them go, and be at peace with our Souls. They need to travel on into the realms of Light, where they can come into a state of grace with God.

Once those loved ones have been escorted into the Light and have had a chance to rest and become whole, they can return again to be with us on the inner plane. Many times my clients witness their loved ones in dreams, or in waking visions, after our work is done. These same clients had not been able to see their deceased loved ones before our work, because of the grief that bound them.

I have witnessed in my meditations with the Angels a darkness wrapped around the world. It weighs heavily on all of us and represents all the sadness and grief of the trapped Souls of children and deceased people who have not been able to enter the realms of Light because of difficult deaths, or because of belief systems that gave them no guidance for reaching the Light.

✦

This is no time for blame. All Ministers and Teachers of all religions need to understand that shunning a woman who has had an abortion is harmful to her and to the child's Soul at a time they need the most help. Women choose this desperate act of abortion for many reasons. The fact that they even had to make the choice is a sad commentary on the state of our society today.

Likewise, every woman who has suffered through a miscarriage, stillbirth or sudden death of her child, needs Spiritual guidance and completion for herself and her child's Soul. In all cases, the men are affected too, whether they know it or not. All parties need to find the peace that comes when releasing the child's Soul into the Light.

Lifting the trapped Earthbound Souls of humanity into the Light allows each family to come into grace. Guilt dissolves as forgiveness is done. Pain is relieved, and then all can come back into true alignment with their Sacred purpose. Forgiveness is the key. It is important to ask for forgiveness for self and for others.

We are a human race with deep connections to each other. Not one of us can stand aside and say this is not our responsibility. Every one of us needs to pray and ask that God's Love be revealed in our hearts and in the hearts of all human kind. We need to reach out to help each other. At the highest level we are all One. We are all aspects of God. How can we not ask for the highest good for everyone? Most Spiritual paths teach that Love is the highest frequency and is the highest form of healing there is. Love crosses all boundaries, all religions and all faiths. Love is the only way, and it is often the thing most lacking in people's lives.

✦

Our thoughts intertwine like a living web around the globe. Those with the gift of sight are able to perceive these thoughts and how they act on the physical human stage. As you think so you create. Fear begets fear. Love begets love.

✦

We each have a choice about how we use our minds to create our world and influence those around us. In this book I have shared my own story and the stories of my clients in order to demonstrate how anger and hate have hurt people, how love and prayer can heal. It is important for each of us to know that the power of our minds can heal or hurt.

Our choice to love or hate affects our whole life. Are we using our minds and hearts to create powerful positive energy for the healing of the planet? Or are we being angry at the world and spending our lives in hate? Are we tuning into violence on television for relaxation when we come home exhausted from work? Or are we choosing Spiritual books and educational programs that will uplift us and prayer work that can heal?

Being tired and relaxed puts us in a very receptive state; therefore, we must all be aware of what we choose to let our minds relax to. Television is a very persuasive medium, as is the internet and radio. We are affected by all that we see and hear. We must ask ourselves what is the prime motive of the media? Is it to entertain? Give us an accurate reflection of the Truth? Or fill our minds with confusion while the real Truth is hidden? Are we being given so much information that we are overwhelmed with irrelevancies while critical global situations are ignored?

The larger the group watching a particular show or involved with a chat forum online, or radio show, the larger the group mind that is beginning to grow and network together. Even if individuals are spread thousands of miles apart and do not know each other, it has a powerful binding effect. It is akin to mass hypnosis. The group mind is being formed and linked with a series of thoughts, images and emotions. Thoughts and emotions have dynamic energy. Leaders and advertisers know this. Repetition has a huge effect on the subconscious mind, hence the continual repeats of emotive advertising.

✦

172

Now more than at any time in the history of humankind massive change can happen in an instant when millions of people decide to act, for better or for worse. We are dynamically connected through all the various forms of electronic communication.

This is a very volatile world.

Think on this for a moment and ask yourself, where do you want to tune your heart and mind to? Where do you want your voice heard? Do you want to co-create with God on a higher level, or are you happy to let your mind be subconsciously run by the media or others? Everything you let your mind take in has an effect on all levels of your Being. Each moment you make the choice on what you focus your mind upon. Your choice links you at a mental level with others according to where your thoughts are directed. Choose carefully.

✦

Prayer does not focus on the negative. It does not look for wrongs or the reasons for blame. It focuses on the affirmation of God within everything. Finding that simple truth and affirming the God in yourself and in all others is the key. Affirm the true perfection of God within you and focus on the Light within your heart. Rekindle that flame of knowing. At Higher Self level you do know this Truth, but if your Soul has been damaged it is often hard to see it. Continued prayer will be answered and Light will come into your heart. The desire for wholeness and being at one with God is what will bring healing to you and your family.

✦

173

A Question of Choice

This chapter is written with love and compassion in my heart to help parents and the Spirit of their child make appropriate choices for the highest good of all involved.

In our lives we are faced with many choices. It is not my desire to tell you what your choices should be. Each individual must weigh all the facts and listen to his or her own heart. It is through the heart center that your Guides, Teachers and Angels will communicate with you. Pay attention to what you feel in your heart before you make decisions about any major steps in your life. In your heart you will know when you are making a bad choice – the heart will feel heavy, sad, fearful or worried. Choices that are right will make your heart feel bright, joyous and happy.

We all need to be fully conscious of, and fully responsible for, the choices we make in life. If a man and a woman have conceived a child and are currently facing difficult decisions, it is time to think about the direction they want to go in their lives. They made many choices even before they conceived. Some of those choices they may have made unconsciously. Whether they were conscious of their choices or not, what they set in motion with those choices has now come into Being in the form of a new life.

If the pregnancy is *not* what they want, it is time for them to respect themselves enough, to take *full* responsibility for all the decisions they made that brought them to this point in their lives. To play a victim role gives their power away to whatever, or whomever, they blame for the situation. By assuming *total* responsibility for their lives, they can claim back their power. They can then recognize that they have always been the ones creating their life-paths through their choices, or lack of them. When they understand this, they will know they have the power, from this day forward, to *consciously* create their lives the way they want. Then they can take the appropriate action for the new life they have created.

A man and a woman should have all the facts in front of them before making the choice to conceive a child and before making a choice to end a pregnancy.

✦

I feel that no woman should be forced to become pregnant or stay pregnant against her will. She should have a choice. It is her body. At the same time she and her mate need to be fully responsible for their choice to terminate a pregnancy, and comprehend the full implications of the choice, before they decide to proceed. This is where Spiritual guidance can help them.

A woman's choice whether to remain pregnant or not reaches far beyond her individual person. She needs to understand how the choice to terminate her pregnancy with an abortion affects her future health, her DNA which records the event as a trauma to her body, all levels of her Being in this life, all her future lives, the health of the father of the child, her family and all the future generations that may come from the child she now carries in her womb. She may never know the true life plan of the child and how his Spirit may have been destined to change the course of history in the world.

A man, or anyone else involved in the woman's life, such as a parent, also needs to consider all of these things. If any of them are forcing a woman to terminate the pregnancy, they will also take on the karma that comes with terminating a life.

✦

We shape our future by our actions in the present. Working from a place of compassion and love we can set up a resonance that will attract similar loving energies back to us that will support us and our family now and in the future. However, negative entanglements of energy between people and the child's Soul before, during, and after an abortion can act in a depleting cycle and go on for lifetimes, affecting the health of all involved.

✦

For too long society has not understood the Truth or the consequences of abortion.

It is my hope that this book has given all people a chance to pause, to reconsider their values and understand the Sacredness of the incoming Spirit of the child.

✦

Conscious conception is the ideal, where both parents are willing to accept the full responsibility of raising a child.

The decision to conceive should be upheld as a Sacred agreement between a man, a woman and the incoming Spirit of the child.

A man and a woman's first and most important choice is with whom they choose to be sexually involved. Both parties need to discuss very seriously the outcome of sex. Love needs to be the basis for any committed, monogamous relationship to succeed. Casual sex without love will only lead to problems, such as unwanted pregnancies, sexually transmitted diseases, and negative psychic energetic entanglements between partners that can last for years or even lifetimes after a relationship has ended.

The choice of a mate is so important. Your energies intermingle and take on each other's influences every time you interact. You affect each other deeply at every level whether you are conscious of it or not.

Fully understanding the implications of terminating an unwanted pregnancy needs to be thought about *before* conception. Sane discussions between a man and a woman need to happen before getting involved sexually. If one thinks that abortion is acceptable and the other does not, then it is time to stop and reconsider the relationship. Only pain can result in such a relationship if pregnancy occurs. Too often pregnancy is not planned or wanted, and then decisions are made under duress and in haste.

✦

Abortion is a poor choice of birth control and not something I would ever want to recommend, as I have seen the long-lasting consequences that go way beyond the loss of the child. This is very serious. As you have witnessed in the case histories in this book, the wounds of losing a child can affect all levels of your Being. The Physical Body can remain in distress for years, unless healing is done and hormones are balanced. The karmic effects may reverberate for lifetimes. Abortion can be even more devastating than miscarriage or stillbirth because of the overlying guilt and anguish that often accompanies it. It should not be entered into without careful consideration.

The contraceptive pill gave men and women a false sense of security. Though it may have prevented many pregnancies, it allowed people to become very casual about relationships and sex. It is not the answer many thought it was. I have heard too many stories of women becoming pregnant while using the pill and/or other methods of birth control. I have also been told that certain antibiotics will cancel out the contraceptive effects of the pill. If children are not wanted in a relationship, then I suggest you seriously review the situation.

There is no fail-safe contraception that I know of other than abstinence, vasectomy, or the removal of the ovaries from the woman. Removal of the ovaries is a not a choice many women would willingly take and can lead to major health problems. Tying the fallopian tubes has not proven to be fail-safe. If a pregnancy would end a relationship, then it is far better to know that ahead of time than when pregnant.

> *Therefore when you are involved sexually, you must always be aware that pregnancy is a strong possibility, no matter which method of contraception is used.*

The more recently developed "morning after pill" has great repercussions that need to be discussed here. Not knowing that you *were* pregnant does not stop a child's Soul from being harmed. I have seen ovaries in women in a very unbalanced, angry state after using this pill and have witnessed women weeping when they realize they were indeed pregnant, and that now with hindsight they had wanted the child. They may have been unconscious at one level that they had conceived, but their Physical Bodies and other levels of their Beings knew it all and would have continued to grieve the loss, if healing and the Soul's release work had not been done.

+

After I was raped and went through the abortion at sixteen, the doctors put me on the contraceptive pill. I stayed on it for about six months and finally could stand the effects no longer. Continuous migraines, bloating and weight gain, swollen and tender breasts, mood swings, depression and nausea made me give it up.

> *I now know that after an abortion or a miscarriage the estrogen/progesterone ratio needed for good health can be thrown off balance. Progesterone can sink too low causing "estrogen dominance."*

Estrogen dominance is a term coined by John. R. Lee, M.D.,[1] to mean the essential ratio between progesterone and estrogen has skewed, and the levels of estrogen are too high for safety. I believe the pill caused a further swing towards estrogen dominance in my body after the abortion. All the symptoms listed above are typical of estrogen dominance and increased alarmingly the longer I took the pill.

> *This information is essential for all women. Estrogen dominance can lead to cancer in the long term.*

Many women have come to me with their hormones in complete disarray after having been on the pill for years. Likewise, women who have been given hormone replacement therapy (HRT) for pre-menopause or menopause have had horrendous results, many coming to me for healing after cancer surgeries. I cannot emphasize enough the importance of balancing the hormones after losing a child, after removal of the ovaries, or after a hysterectomy *even* if ovaries are left, as the operation invariably reduces the blood supply to the ovaries, causing them to function below normal and eventually atrophy. As I said at the beginning of this book, I am not a doctor so I do not prescribe. However, I do encourage all women to take responsibility for their bodies and do their own research on these critical issues.

Natural, pure progesterone is available and may help you balance your hormones after the loss of a child, but be sure to get a cream that has the right quality and strength.

---

[1] *See Dr. Lee's books in the Reference Section to understand the full impact of hormones and health.*

The synthetic form of progesterone called progestin is not a good option and has many negative side effects. Likewise, synthetic estrogens used in HRT are very disruptive to the body.

During menopause, although estrogen levels get low, progesterone can drop to zero, leaving the body out of balance, creating estrogen dominance. The ratio between these two hormones is critical for good health. You may need both hormones to be balanced under the guidance of a good doctor.

If you feel you need estrogen or progesterone, please review Dr. Lee's books listed in the Reference Section for natural sources and important information on how to use the creams. Or go to my website[2] for sources of natural progesterone and estrogen creams that I have found useful. Always seek your doctor's advice when dealing with hormones but be sure that doctor is aware of the dangers of synthetic hormones. Dr. Lee's books are essential reading on these issues and may save your life.

Ever since the contraceptive pill was introduced, women have been led to believe they were safe using it. We have yet to see the long-term effects on the children who have been born to women who once used the pill. How will their offspring and future generations be affected? Also I have to question the use of powerful fertility drugs that force the ovaries to ripen more than one egg at a time. There have been recent reports that the women who used these drugs fifteen years ago to conceive are now dying of cancer. What damage is done to the eggs so unnaturally forced along by these drugs, and what is the subsequent damage to the hormonal balance of the children so conceived? How will they be affected as adults?

Hormonal imbalance can be a major cause of depression.

What worries me now is the number of women being treated for depression with Prozac and other similar drugs such as Paxil. Sarafem is basically the same as Prozac in another coating and being touted as useful for female conditions such as PMS. This has dangerous implications. Women do not necessarily know they are being given an anti-depressant

---

[2] *My website is www.angelsoflightandhealing.org*

when Sarafem is handed to them. These drugs do not handle the underlying hormonal imbalance that may be the cause of the depression and PMS, and can critically change the brain chemistry. Some women are being kept on Prozac throughout pregnancy by their doctors, because a sudden withdrawal from the drug can create massive mood swings and even suicide. I refer you to Dr. Ann Blake Tracy's book *Prozac, Panacea or Pandora?* and to her web site listed in the Reference Section for full details on this. She has found a tremendous increase in the numbers of autistic children being born to women using Prozac and other similar anti-depressant drugs. Dr. Tracy reports that the alarming increase in autism correlates precisely with the timing of the introduction of this class of drugs to the market. This is devastating news, if it is indeed true. Dr. Tracy also suggests that the use of these drugs may be implicated in the rapid rise of obesity and diabetes nationwide.

> *If you are using any of this class of drugs, do not come off them quickly. It can be very dangerous. Please listen to Dr. Tracy's tape[3] on how to withdraw safely from these drugs. If you are using these anti-depressants, I would suggest you avoid pregnancy until you have completely cleared your system of the drug residues.*

We must all become aware of the health risks that come from being unconscious of our choices. We must wake up to what is happening and choose what is right for our own health, our children's health and the health of generations to come.

> *Changing your mind part way through a pregnancy may have serious, long-term effects on your health.*

> *I believe that a woman, her partner (if he is available and supportive) and the Spirit of their child should all have a choice about the continuation of a pregnancy.*

---

[3] *Ann Blake Tracy, Ph.D., is a leading researcher into the effects of SSRI antidepressants. Her contact address and book and tape information are listed in the Reference Section.*

I also strongly believe that this choice should be made understanding all the information presented in this book and in traditional Sacred Texts.

> *It is important to remember the child's Spirit can be, and should be, spoken to gently at all times during the pregnancy. The Spirit is a conscious, living Being.*

✦

> *Let us review your choices in handling an unexpected pregnancy.*

The first choice would be to know and recognize that the incoming Spirit is a precious gift from God and should be kept within the family matrix. There is a reason this child has come to you; there may be many lifetimes you have shared. I would ask both parents to sit quietly and think about what agreements they may have to birth this child's Spirit in this life. This Spirit may have helped you in another life and may be your best friend. Perhaps you owe this Spirit a debt and this is your chance to repay her. Perhaps the pregnancy was not planned consciously at the mental level in this life, but at Spirit level this may have been exactly what you agreed to many centuries ago.

✦

However, I am fully aware of all the conditions a woman may find herself in that do not easily allow for a pregnancy to continue. She may be in a violent household. Her physical Being and the child may be at risk. She may have a health condition or severe financial worries that make her feel it impossible for her to go forward with a pregnancy. Then, she needs to consider all her options. If she is in a violent relationship, is the relationship worth staying in if she and the child are at risk? Could she support herself and the child financially in other ways? Are there other family members that could help? Could she remain pregnant safely in the household and then give the child up for adoption? Would her overall physical and mental health handle the stress of the unplanned pregnancy? Are there any Spiritual counselors that can help her nearby?

✦

If you find yourself at an impasse at this point, prayer can be a powerful tool if you approach it with an open heart and mind. If calling on God,

182

Christ, Mary or the Angels is not something you have done before, please know they are available to you and can help. By requesting help at this time to be shown a way forward, ways may be revealed to you that will allow you to proceed in grace. When you ask for help, then the universe can respond. You may be surprised at the way things can work out for you.

I believe that if a woman and her partner lovingly contact their child's Spirit, they will choose the appropriate action. Just knowing the child has a Spirit and a consciousness is a huge step towards making the right decision.

Many great Teachers are wishing to be born at this critical time in the humanity's history; you can be sure your child is important, no matter what part he or she is to play.

✦

Still, sometimes parents may feel they cannot handle a pregnancy for their own private reasons. If this is your choice, then please give the child's Spirit a choice to stay or leave.

If both parents are *absolutely sure* they do not want to continue the pregnancy, they should both speak with love from their hearts to the child's Spirit with clear intent and explain the reasons they believe they cannot proceed. If a woman finds herself facing pregnancy having been abandoned by the father of the child, she should do this work alone with the child's Spirit, or she may ask a Spiritual counselor to help her.

It is important to do this prayer work and have the discussion with the child's Spirit as early as possible. The "Forgiveness Prayer" will help dissolve any negativity between you, but it is your discussion with the Spirit that is the key to letting the Spirit know your situation, so the Spirit can take appropriate action. Ambivalence and changing your mind will only tangle your energies. If you are ambivalent, it may be a sign that you really do not want to terminate the pregnancy and your Angels, Guides and Teachers are trying to speak to you through your heart. For some of you, this may be the only chance to have a child in this life. Review your options again thoroughly.

Please remember, you are not threatening an abortion or giving an ultimatum, you are requesting the child's Spirit reconsider his life plan with you and that he reviews the situation for the highest good of all. This review is exactly what you should be doing also. You can at this time choose to offer the child's Spirit a new body at a better period in your life, so that no karma is unfinished between you, the child, and humanity. Remember, the timing of this child's birth may be critical for this period of humanity's evolution. Even if you cannot see your child's Spirit in front of you, he will be right there and hear you. Stay in a peaceful, prayerful state, so that you will be able to hear or feel any guidance from your Angels, Guides and Teachers. The "Prayer of Light" in the next section of this book will keep your mind focused on the Divine Source within you and will help at this time.

✦

Speaking with your child's Spirit is no different than talking with an adult. Speak directly to the Spirit as if he or she is standing in front of you. You should communicate gently and lovingly with the child's Spirit from your heart and request that he or she reconsider the timing of the pregnancy. This gives the child's Spirit a chance to work with you. Though the Physical Body of the child may be small, the over-lighting Spirit is an intelligent Being of Light that has existed for aeons and is very wise. Remember, the Spirit created the Soul a long time ago. It is the Soul that carries much of the damage of previous lifetimes. However, from what I have seen both the Spirit's link to the Soul *and* the Soul itself can be damaged during an abortion, unless they can withdraw safely beforehand.

✦

As you saw in my case at the beginning of this book, my husband was angry about my being pregnant. I knew that both the child and myself were in danger if I was to stay pregnant, so I spoke gently with the child's Spirit. This Spirit had just witnessed the anger of my husband and clearly understood his position. I softly asked the child's Spirit to reconsider, as I did not want him to be hurt by such violence as I had seen. I thanked this beautiful Spirit for coming to us. I could see that he was a very special Being of Light. He acknowledged me with a clear, sweet look and bowed his head, graciously, letting me know he understood. With that, he easily withdrew the cord of Light that connected his Spirit and Soul to the tiny embryo in my womb. He returned to the Light with the Angels, his Spirit gradually fading away from my view. The whole conversation lasted less than five minutes. Within half an hour my period came down. There was no pain and no trauma for either of us, for two reasons: it was an early term pregnancy; my period was only two weeks beyond the due date; and I did not hold onto my child's energy as he left. I let him go with sincere love in my heart.

I cannot say whether a transition such as this will go so easily for other women. I do know this has to be done with love and no regrets, as any negative emotion will hold the child back, because negative energy acts like a black sticky cord around the child's Being. My husband's anger had not apparently stopped our child's Spirit from leaving, perhaps because he had only minutes before found out about the pregnancy from me. He did not have much time to brew over it and create a huge negative field towards the child. The table he had pounded on took much of the focus of his rage. Once I had agreed to talk with our child, my husband became quiet. Much of his anger left while he listened to me speaking to the child's Spirit. I was also sending the Spirit a strong beam of love and Light from my heart throughout the whole process, and I was aware of many Angels with us protecting us in the Light.

> *Allowing the child to peacefully return to the Light under his own volition very early in the pregnancy is by far the safest and happiest way to proceed if the timing is not right for birth. No harm will be done. The child's Spirit is then free to choose to return to you later if that is your wish, or he or she may choose to be born to others. Using the "Forgiveness Prayer" will help at this time to release any karma that has been created between you. I did not know the prayer at the time but loving communication with the child's Spirit was apparently all he needed to understand the situation. Perhaps this more than anything in this book helps you understand the wisdom of your child.*

Even a damaged Soul will hear you speak to him. Though he may have forgotten his contact with the Spiritual realms, his Spirit has not left him. The Soul just does not remember that Divine part of himself after all the lifetimes of trauma he has seen. You can be sure that no child wants to go through the pain of abortion. Most would certainly choose an easier path.

✦

The ease of leaving will depend upon the karmic connections, and/ or emotional entanglements parents have created with the child, and on the importance of the birth to that child, who may not want to let go. This might be his only opportunity to be with you in this lifetime. Using the "Forgiveness Prayer" will help release many of these entanglements so that you can all see and feel more clearly what needs to be done. Please try to see, hear and feel the child's Spirit response to you with an open heart. Try to understand his or her needs also.

The karmas that bind you and your child may be such that it is not easy for the child to leave of his own volition, in which case perhaps you need to reconsider. This may be a very important chance to complete karmic debts between you. If your child's Spirit has not been able to easily leave for any reason, then listen to your heart's knowing about it and continue praying for an answer.

If you proceed lovingly throughout this process, the child will not be traumatized, so do not feel you have damaged the Soul by gently requesting he reconsider. He will be grateful you gave him a choice to review his options. Also, if you have had any negative thoughts about being pregnant, please do not feel you have damaged a Soul beyond repair and should therefore abort him. You can help the Soul heal by surrounding him with Love and Christ Light, and using the "Forgiveness Prayer." Uplifting prayers should be done throughout any pregnancy to bring the healing Light of Love around yourself and the child. Being at peace with the pregnancy if you decide to remain pregnant will help the child's Soul heal.

✦

Please wait at least three days before proceeding with any other action after speaking with your child's Spirit and continue your prayers throughout that time. Give your child's Spirit a chance to decide.

If your child's Spirit decides to remove his or her life force from the embryo and return to the Light, you will have a natural miscarriage. It is important to continue the prayer work to help him throughout his transition with the prayers in the next section of this book.

✦

I am encouraged by my Angels and Guides to add this very important point: no man should treat a woman harshly if she miscarries a child.

I would be greatly distressed to think that a man would take this information and blame a woman for a miscarriage if that woman sincerely wanted the child, and it had not been their conscious choice for the child to leave. A sudden, unexpected miscarriage can be a painful, heart-breaking affair for all involved. A woman needs great love and support during this time, as does the child's Soul. Remember there are many situations that can cause a miscarriage, all listed in previous chapters. The man's input has as much effect upon the child's Spirit as the woman's. This is why I have repeated that all parties should be lovingly involved during a pregnancy if it is to come to full term. More particularly love needs to be the keynote after the loss of a child so that the transition of the child's Soul can be with grace. Anger or blame will hold the Soul back and will damage the family matrix. Forgiveness of all parties is essential.

✦

If your child's Spirit is not able to leave during the three days, then once again you need to seriously reconsider. Only you can choose; no one can do this for you. This is your Sacred journey. Your Angels and Guides and Teachers are beside you and will help you make the right decisions if you will listen with your heart. You will not hear them or feel your heart's true knowing if you are in a fearful or angry state of mind. Use the "Prayer of Light" to help you focus your heart. You cannot avoid the lessons that are in front of you. You played your part in creating them. Any negative thoughts of suicide, blaming others, or making others pay will only compound your lessons at this time. I speak from experience. I have been there. Face your situation with as much grace and honesty as you can muster. This is where it is important to take full responsibility for your actions.

After all the work I have done with women over the years, and the great compassion I have for them in facing their difficult situations, I still find myself working hard to understand the whole picture from the greater perspective of the wonderful Teachers of Light who work with me. This section of the book has been the hardest for me to write, as I know women sometimes face truly desperate situations. I have been there myself.

I wanted to help women face what they must face, give them a choice, and help the child's Spirit be free, to somehow make it easier for them all. But what my Teachers are explaining to me is that all of us, every minute of each day, are making choices that draw to us our experiences. We are creating our destiny, individually *and* globally, as a part of the Greater Human Consciousness. We have chosen our lessons to learn by. I cannot take any lesson or karma away from you or make it easy, neither can the Angels, it is how you have chosen to grow Spiritually. Had I not worked through my difficult life lessons, I could not teach you what I have learned. There is a great cosmic law working here.

A woman finds herself pregnant because of a natural law. It is no accident. She chose to be where she was when she became pregnant. Something drew her and the man to that place in time and space to conceive, whether it was karmic, his desire, or hers. For every action there is a reaction. That is the law of karma.

What we hold in our hearts and minds as our main focus is what we draw to us.

✦

I have often looked back on that fearful night when I was raped and left in the snow. I know, with hindsight, that I did not have to go through rape. There had been a friend at the dance who was going to leave early at nine o'clock. I could have gone with her, but I chose to stay and have more fun. By staying late and dancing in that rowdy nightclub, I set the stage for being preyed upon. Energies run heavy, dark and sensual in nightclubs. Alcohol blurs judgment. Though I did not drink, I knew the eighteen-year-old youth that I danced with towards the end of the evening was drinking heavily. I let my guard down because he was good looking and I had often admired him at a distance, on the rugby field at school. I admit I was attracted to him. But also I felt warning signs of fear in my heart, which I chose to ignore. Those warning signs I have come to pay great attention to, but at that time I did not realize how very serious things were about to become. I danced with him only once and then went looking for my friends in the band for a ride home, but they had no space left in their cars. The dance hall was emptying fast. It was midnight and I began to panic that I would not have a ride home. There were only a few people left in sight and none that I knew. It was the drunk who offered me a ride home. Against my better judgement I agreed as he seemed to be the only option left. I had no money for a taxi with me. I could have made a collect call home but did not want to bother my mother so late or admit I had made a mistake. Every action I took that night led to what happened. I played my part in the drama. Probably there were a thousand or more other outcomes I could have chosen.

It was many years until I could finally see the Truth that I was as much in control of that drama as the drunk I chose to spend my time with. *I was no victim.* I did not have to stay late, dance with him, or accept the ride he offered. This does not in any way let him off the very serious offence of rape, but forgiving him and myself set me free. Any man who forces sex upon a woman or a young person will have to face very serious karmic repercussions for his actions. This karma cannot be avoided and will come full circle with what appears to me to be exact mathematical precision, no matter how many lifetimes need to pass by. Energies misued are lost in an event until a chance comes to retrieve them and redeem them with forgiveness and grace.

A woman must answer her own questions about unwanted sex by listening to her heart and asking what part did she play in the situation leading up to the event. Only she can decide what her response should be to a pregnancy coming from this kind of situation. For myself, almost thirty-four years later, having finally spoken with my own child's Spirit on this subject, I now know why she chose to come to me. She came as a friend to help me at that difficult time. She has forgiven me, and I her, for all that took place. By recognizing my part in that whole drama and forgiving myself and all involved, I was able to take my life back.

I have explained this so that any man or woman considering abortion will pause to think. The pregnancy happened for a reason, based on your choices. What you choose to do now will change your life again.

⊹

In discussion with Christ, Mary and all my Guides, Teachers and Angels, they insist here strongly that abortion should not be considered, for the great damage it does to the whole human race. These great Beings weep each time a child dies this way. They weep for all involved, as they know the long-term consequences of abortion for everyone.

✦

This does not take away your individual right to choose, but it does put it in a very different light. The child is a living Being and part of the Greater Consciousness of Humanity. Whatever damage is done to the child's Soul reverberates in the Greater Soul of Humanity.

✦

Some parents may still feel they need to make the very difficult choice to terminate a pregnancy with an abortion. Then they must both be responsible for their decision. In the end, however, the real burden falls upon the woman. She is the one agreeing to the procedure. Whether she has been forced into it or not by her mate or her family, she does have the ultimate say. It is her body. This puts tremendous pressure on her.

If you are making this choice, then it is very important to make sure that prayers are done before, during and after the procedure to assist the child's Soul in his or her transition.

Without proper care and Spiritual guidance, your child's Soul may not be able to reach the Light. Your pure, loving intent is what is needed with the help of Christ, Mary and the Angels to guide the Soul's return to the Light. All this work must be done in a Sacred way, treating the child with great respect as a living Spiritual Being.

As you have read in the case histories, if a child's Soul is not able to break free before an abortion, he or she will need healing and love to be able to return to the Light. This work may need to be done with the help of a Spiritual healer if the damage is great. The healer can also make sure the child's Soul is safely released from your Being and from the child's father, or anyone else that may be holding the Soul back. The later the abortion takes place, the greater the damage that is done to the woman and the child's Soul. What can bind a Soul is grief, anger, guilt, or any other negative emotions between the parents and the Soul of the child. This may also include old karmic ties from previous lives. Being angry with the child will only prevent the Soul from leaving and bind you further. Unconditional love and forgiveness between all parties will help the child's Soul be free.

I caution you here, not to use the prayers in the following section with a casual attitude just before an abortion, assuming your child's Soul will reach the Light. No one should ever think that abortion is acceptable because they quickly repeated the "Forgiveness Prayer" and the "Transitional Prayer" beforehand. The child's Soul may not be able to leave if prayers are not spoken with love, compassion and forgiveness. Your body and the child's Soul may as a result, suffer the long-term consequences of the unhealed wounds. The prayers should be spoken with uplifting love from your heart and full understanding of what they represent, calling upon Christ, Mary and the Angels to assist the child. Even with that understanding it is sometimes hard for the Soul to leave before the abortion, as you saw in Jen's case. She was under pressure to have the abortion and in her heart she could not let go of her child's Spirit.

These prayers are given to assist you in a time of great need. They are given to you with love in the sincere hope that the child's Soul will be helped in this time of transition. Please do not think that I am saying abortion is an acceptable choice if you use these prayers. Every abortion takes a toll on each person involved far greater than you can imagine. I am offering these prayers only because I know there will always be some women who will choose abortion, believing it truly is their only option, and I do not want to see the continued pain of their children's Souls nor the continued pain of the parents. Abortion is a very serious event. At this point you know the Truth and you are responsible for what you do with it. This whole book is a wake-up call for everyone. Now you have this information you need to act upon it with great responsibility.

Before proceeding with an abortion you should have already gently spoken to your child's Spirit with love, explaining your reasons for not continuing the pregnancy, and you should have given the Spirit a chance to withdraw his or her life force for at least three days before proceeding with any action. You should be using all the prayers in the next section to prepare yourself and the child. The child's Spirit should be informed of any decisions that affect his or her Physical Body, so that he or she can be prepared and take appropriate action. Ask that Christ, Mary and the Angels be with the child to help in the transition. Continue your prayers before, during and after the abortion to help your child's Soul be free and help yourself heal.

In some situations, as in the case of Margaret, who had been exposed to X-rays in early pregnancy, the choice is made for medical reasons. Margaret had not wanted the abortion, but her doctors advised it was for the best. Margaret knew enough to uplift the Spirit of her child in loving prayer and explained to the child what needed to be done, and why, before the abortion took place. At the same time she had welcomed the child back as soon as she was able to return. The child's Spirit was able to leave and call back the Soul's energy without any apparent trauma, before the abortion. Margaret became pregnant again, as was her wish, the very next month with the same Spirit as her child. Her child could then continue her destiny in this life as planned. Thus no negative karma resulted.

Please be gentle with yourself, and your child's Soul.

✦

A Special Note to Doctors, Nurses, Healthcare Workers and Counselors

I was forty-eight before I finally realized why I was not able to fully heal from the abortion at age sixteen. Finally I went back in meditation to the time of the surgery and found that the doctors and nurses had said and thought many negative things about me during the abortion, while I was under general anesthesia. They probably had no idea I had been raped. Their thoughts had lodged in my Being and had a very negative impact on my system. My child's Soul had not been able to leave until many years after the abortion, when I was twenty-eight, and I had used the homeopathic remedy "Staphysagria." That seemed to allow my body to complete the pregnancy at a non-physical level and release the emotional trauma to a certain degree, which allowed the Soul's release. It was thirty-two years after the abortion when I used the "Forgiveness Prayer" in my meditation that I was finally able to release the negative thought forms of the doctors and nurses from my Being, disentangle my energy from the event, and return back to my child's Soul what belonged to her in that timeline.

Anytime we interact, we affect each other's Beings. This is particularly important for practitioners to understand when counseling a patient or during procedures of any kind. Doctors and nurses must be very careful of their thoughts, feelings and what they verbalize, as the patient is in a very receptive and open state of mind, especially if under general anesthesia.

I would ask that you gently share the information in this book with all women at least three days before they go through any procedure to terminate a pregnancy, to allow them time to reconsider and speak with their child's Spirit. If it is still their choice to proceed, then the prayer work should be done before, during, and after the procedure to help the child's

Soul reach the Light, preferably with a Spiritual healer who understands the process.

It is essential to hold the mother and the child in an attitude of love and ask that Christ, Mary and the Angels be there to assist them both. This is a very difficult time for them. Treat them with great care. We may never know the full reasons behind the woman's decision. Her choice may affect her for a long time to come. Be sure that your energies are not compounding her problems.

> *Please help the child's Soul make his or her transition in peace with prayers.*

✦

A Special Note to All Women
Who Have Had an Abortion

It is time to heal yourself, your child's Soul and your family. You had a very difficult choice to make. Choose to heal and resolve any anger or sadness about the situation. Forgive yourself and forgive everyone involved, including the father of the child, family members, and any doctors, nurses or counselors that may have affected your choice. Your child's Soul cannot easily return to the Light if you are holding any negative emotions about the situation. Forgiveness is the key.

Bring your Light to the world with Love in your heart. Lift your child's Soul to the Light and be free. The following prayers in the next section will help you. Remember the Creator does not reject any of us; we only reject ourselves when we forget our own Spiritual Destiny and our Sacred Inner Spirit.

> *I ask Christ, Mary and the Angels now to help all parents*
> *and their children who had to face such a difficult choice.*
> *May their Souls be free and their hearts be full.*

✦

A Special Note to All Women Who Have Lost a Child

The prayers in the next section will help you no matter how your child was lost. Be at peace with yourself and know healing is available for you, your family, and your child's Soul. Many Angels are waiting to assist you now as you proceed to the next section to do your prayer work. You can be sure that Christ and Mary will be there for you also if you call on them. That is their promise as I write these words. Already the Light is around you.

Proceed in grace and be gentle with your self. Forgive yourself and all parties involved.

Certain homeopathics, essential oils, and flower remedies may assist you at this time with the physical and emotional healing. Please review the Reference Section for details. I found that the homeopathic remedy, "Staphysagria," was a tremendous help and allowed my body a completion of each pregnancy at a non-physical level. It was this that helped release both Souls of my two lost children from my Being. The Angels could then take them into the Light. Years later I found essential oils were also very valuable for healing and seemed to help resolve my emotional pain at a level the homeopathic did not reach. The Bach Flower remedy "Star of Bethlehem" helped me resolve feelings of deep loss and allowed the grieving process to be complete.

You may choose to use these remedies, but most importantly you must forgive yourself and everyone involved.

PART IV.

PRAYERS OF FORGIVENESS AND TRANSITION

THE SACRED RITES

✦

The Prayer Work Begins

Standing with your feet firmly planted on the ground, put your hands together in prayer against your heart. This will help you focus your intent on the heart center, and harmonize your body's frequency. Breathe quietly and relax. Quiet your mind by watching your own gentle breathing.

Be at peace in your Soul. This work will help you come into a deeper state of grace and will allow you to become whole. It will also help you let go of sadness from loss.

✦

Opening the Sacred Space

You are now going to request the Divine Presence of all the Angels, Guides and Teachers, and Beings of Light in service to God. These Beings will work with you, if you call upon them with an open heart. Treat them with the utmost respect and thank each one as you ask them to assist you. You may see or feel their presence as they come in, but don't worry if you do not notice anything as it takes a while to become accustomed to this higher sensitivity.

I ask that the Archangels, Michael, Gabriel, Uriel and Raphael be with me.

The Archangels will come and stand at the four quadrants around you to protect your Sacred prayer work.

I ask that my Guides and Teachers, Guardian Angels and the Healing Angels be with me.

You have many Guides and Teachers that work every day with you in addition to your Guardian Angels. The Healing Angels are available to anyone who needs special help with healing work if they are called upon,

I ask that Lord Jesus Christ and Mother Mary be with me.

I never begin any healing work without these two wonderful healers beside me. I always see Christ on my left and Mary on my right. You may also include whichever Spiritual teachers you choose to work with here.

I ask that the over-lighting Angel of this Place be with me.

Every place has an Angel assigned to it. It is always good to acknowledge their presence and include them in the work, as they can greatly assist you. Hospitals may have many Angels working, but always there is one Master Angel of Place above the group. Towns and cities have many Angels over-lighting them. Reach to the Angel over-lighting the space you are working in.

God is with me.

You are reaffirming God is with you. You cannot be separate from God. God is your Source from which all healing comes.

Mother Earth please bless this work.

You are asking that the Spirit of Mother Earth bless this work. She is the Sacred ground on which you stand. She represents the mother of all Beings on Earth. It is from the elements of Mother Earth that our Physical Bodies take their sustenance in the form of food and water. She is a magnificent Spiritual Being in her own right.

I ask that a golden sphere of Light be placed around me.

You are asking for a Sacred sphere of protection to be placed around the space in which you will work. Visualize a golden sphere of Light at least the size of the room you are working in being placed around you directly from the Creator Source. The Angels, Christ and Mary will help you do this.

I ask that the healing Light of Christ come into my heart, mind, body and Spirit, and that this work be done for the highest good of all, in accordance with God's Holy Laws.

Here you are asking for purification, and you are committing to abide by God's Holy Laws in the work. Remember this is about healing all parties. It is not about driving a Soul away from you.

I ask that this whole sphere be filled with the Light of Christ, the Light of Love, the Light of Compassion and Healing, the Light of God.

Here you are requesting purification of the Sacred space in which you will work. This is important, as places are often filled with old emotional residues that need to be cleansed.

Amen. So be it.

This affirms that your prayer and Sacred space have been completed.

✦

Once you have called everyone in, you may be seated if you like. I always stand at the beginning in respect to those I am calling upon.

✦

The "Prayer of Light"[1] is a prayer I use at the beginning and end of each day. It was taught to me by the Angels, as were all the prayers in this section. I use this prayer with each of my clients as they come into conscious union with their Higher Self.

As you speak these words, feel the Light enter your Being. Know you are one with that Light, and that you are truly blessed and in God's own heart. It is important that you love yourself. If you do not love yourself, you cannot truly love God, or any other person. If you get stuck on the words "I love myself," keep repeating them until you can say them easily. Let any tears flow that need to flow until you can say, "I love myself," and believe it.

Visualize the golden Light of God pouring in through the top of your head, cascading down into your heart and filling your whole Being. Focus on your heart as you speak these words and see it becoming brighter and brighter until it is like a radiant sun filling your whole body with Light.

✦

---

[1] *The "Prayer of Light" is fully explained in my book "The Angels' Guide to Living on Earth." See Reference Section for details.*

The Prayer of Light

I am the Light,

I serve the Light,

I love the Light,

I love myself,

I love God,

I am one with God.

Use the "Prayer of Light" before beginning your work to focus your Spiritual heart. If you have trouble believing you are a part of God, and One with Him, or that you are worthy to call on Him, then understand there is no part of your Being that is not a part of God. God does not reject any part of you. You only need to forgive yourself and anyone who has hurt you in any way, in order to remove the energies that block this knowing. So pray with faith in your heart, and you will be assisted by the Angels, Christ and Mary as soon as you ask for their help.

You can use this next prayer, the "Forgiveness Prayer,"[2] to forgive any situation that has occurred between you and another person that has caused hurt. For the release work of a deceased Soul, speak directly to them as if they were present and in front of you. Even if you cannot see them, they are usually close by, drawn to you by your thoughts about them. You can cover any difficulties

---

[2] *The "Forgiveness Prayer" is fully explained in my book "The Angels' Guide to Forgiveness." See Reference Section for details.*

you may have had with them and tell them you are sorry. Then use the "Forgiveness Prayer."

If you are helping someone as a client or friend to clear the loss of a child, it is most important that they speak the words of the "Forgiveness Prayer" themselves. Their spoken word is what will begin the healing for all involved. It is their conscious commitment to healing, and their verbal command, that give the Angels, Christ and Mary permission to begin the work. Also, if the other parent is not physically available, I ask the parent who is present to do forgiveness with them using the same prayer (as often there is blame towards the other party.) I also ask them to say the "Forgiveness Prayer" on behalf of the child they conceived with that other party.

The prayer may be repeated as many times as the client feels is necessary, according to how many people were involved in a situation. In this case, you will replace the word "me" with the name of the person you are requesting the departed Soul to forgive.

For example, you may say, "I ask that you forgive *all family members*, or *my husband* and that *they forgive you*."
I find it really helps to speak each line clearly and then have your client repeat it, so they need not worry about reading and can fully focus on their heart's intent to forgive, as you hold the Sacred space for them.

If you are doing this alone for the release of your own child, then proceed slowly and give yourself time to think about each word you speak. See the energies you are releasing back to the child become transmuted as Christ Light, as they return to the child's Soul. Likewise, see your energies return to you, as Christ Light from the child, and see the same for the other parent, so that each person receives back that which is theirs pure and whole. Do this with love and forgiveness in your heart, and the Angels, Christ and Mary will help you.

✦

The Forgiveness Prayer

Before beginning the prayer itself, state who it is you wish to heal.
I ask that this healing work be done for *(name/s of person you wish to be healed.)*

(Here put the name/s of the person/s, or child to be healed. If no name is known for a child, then identify the child to be healed. For example, you may say "my child that was aborted" or "my child that miscarried," or "myself, my family and our stillborn child." Create your own statement that is most appropriate.)

✦

_____

(Here speak the name of the child or person to be forgiven and from whom you seek forgiveness.)

I forgive you for whatever happened between us in this lifetime or any other.

I ask that you forgive me for whatever happened between us in this lifetime or any other.

I ask that God, Christ and Mary, my Guides and Teachers, my Angels and all people forgive me.

I forgive myself.

I ask that the sword of Archangel Michael pass between us so that this can be a clean transition.

I ask that what is truly yours is returned to you as Christ Light, complete and whole, from all levels of my Being, all lifetimes, all the way through DNA and all timelines.

I ask that what is truly mine is returned to me as Christ Light, complete and whole from all levels of your Being, all lifetimes, all the way through DNA and all timelines.

I ask that the Angels and Christ help you reintegrate that which is truly yours as healing Christ Light back into your Being.

I ask that the Angels and Christ help me reintegrate that which is truly mine as healing Christ Light back into my Being.

(If this prayer is being used for forgiveness with a living person, and you are not taking a Soul into the Light, then end with the closing of all doorways in space and time, and the sealing of your auric field, as detailed at the end of this chapter. Otherwise, proceed now to the "Transitional Prayer.")

✦

✦

I use the "Transitional Prayer" to help the Souls of children reach the Light. You can adapt the prayer for any Souls needing help.

(Unless you are a highly trained Spiritual practitioner do not attempt to do transitional work with difficult Earthbound Souls who need special help. That is a whole other work and not covered in this book.)

Always use the "Forgiveness Prayer" first before using the "Transitional Prayer." It is the forgiveness between you that allows the emotional cords to be released.

Use the following prayer for your child, family members or friends that you know need help, adapting the words to suit the situation. When working with adults, I do not request that Mary hold them in her arms; I only request that the Light of Christ enter their Souls in healing.

✦

The Transitional Prayer

I ask now that Mother Mary take this child *(here state the name of child if known)* **in her arms and that the healing Light of Christ, the Light of Love heal all wounds.**

See in your mind's eye golden Christ Light entering into the child's small body gradually awakening it from its sleep. This is when gentleness and love in your heart is most important. As the child's Soul awakens, he/she may well go through the memories of his/her own last death. Be very gentle and see the Light of Love gently healing all wounds until the Soul is bright and free of all darkness and fear.

I ask that God forgive this child and that this child forgive God.

This is important, as many times a child's Soul may be angry with God for what has happened until he/she becomes more aware of the healing Light around him/her.

I ask that this child forgive anyone that has hurt him/her in any lifetime, and that he/she be forgiven for any hurts he/she caused others in any lifetime.

You are covering anything that may have happened that has held the child's Soul back in previous lifetimes, and are asking that forgiveness be done. You have already covered your own forgiveness with the child in the "Forgiveness Prayer," but you may ask again for forgiveness if you wish.

I ask that this child forgive himself/ herself.

This again is important, as the child may be angry at himself/ herself for any number of reasons.

I ask that two or more Angels gently take this child into the Light, to the first level for further healing.

By now the child is most likely awake and can see and hear you. As the child is prepared to leave, you may speak your own words to him/her. Say what you need to say to clear your heart and let him/her go gently into the Light with the Angels. The first level is where all newly-departed Souls go for balancing before moving on to higher realms. Many Healing Angels are present at this level and will assist the Soul in the healing process.

Watch as the child is lifted by the Angels into the Light. If you cannot see the Spiritual realms, then see if you can feel or hear what is happening. Allow a few minutes to pass for the Angels to do their work. I always see the Angels lifting the child to the Heavens. At a certain moment I see golden hands of Light reaching down to carry the child gently upwards. One could say they are the hands of God. Once I see the hands I know the work is almost done. As the Angels and child pass through the gateways to the other realms, I speak the following words:

As this child passes into the Light we give thanks that this is done, and I ask that this doorway be closed in space and time. Amen. So be it.

Then I seal the door to that level by making the sign of a cross in golden Christ Light and the work is done. It is important to seal the doorways after this work is done so that your Soul (or the Soul of your client) is not pulled away from the physical plane but remains firmly in the present moment. If you do not seal the doorways, illness can occur later as part of your Soul may be attempting to stay with the child.

✦

Closing the Time Doorways
and the Sacred Space

It is important to close all doorways on all the work you have been doing once the prayer work has been done. First, request that any residual energy belonging to anyone else that you may have been working with at long distance be returned to them as Christ Light.

I ask that whatever energy belongs to anyone else in this Sacred space is gathered up and returned to them as Christ Light, pure and whole, and I ask that the Angels and Christ help each person reintegrate that which is truly theirs as healing Christ Light.

This may be energy from other family members you included in the prayer work, for example. It is always good to cover your bases by doing this after prayer work, as you do not necessarily know who else may have been drawn to the work you were doing. The Angels will take care of it for you as you request this to be done.

I ask that whatever residual energy belongs to me is gathered up from this Sacred space and returned to me as Christ Light, pure and whole.

See your energy in the Sacred space around you gathered up and returned to your open hands as golden Christ Light and place it back into your heart. This is your own life force; you do not want to leave it behind.

210

I ask that all doorways in space and time be now closed on the work that was done.

With this the Angels will close all doorways.

I ask that my auric field be sealed with the Light of Christ.

With this you are asking the Angels and Christ to help you seal your own energy field.

Now it is time to thank all those who have helped you. Acknowledge each one by name just as you did when you called them in to help you. Stand up and place your hands in prayer against the heart as you speak these words.

I thank everyone for their help in this work.
Archangels, Michael, Gabriel, Uriel and Raphael.
All of the Healing Angels.
My guides and teachers and Guardian Angels.

If you are working with another person thank their guides and teachers and Guardian Angels also, and any belonging to the departed Soul.

Lord Jesus Christ and Mother Mary.

Include any other Spiritual Teachers here that you called upon.

The over-lighting Angel of this Place.
Lord God Almighty and Mother Earth.
I thank you all.

I ask that Christ, Mary and the Angels now dissolve the golden sphere of Light and return it as Christ Light to the Source.

See the sphere dissolve into Christ Light as it returns to God.

I give thanks that the work is done. Amen. So be it.

These words seal the work in your Being and make it final. It confirms with God and all those working with you, that you believe and acknowledge the Sacred completion of this work.

✦

✦

Congratulations, you have just completed a major step in your healing process and in the healing of the world.

✦

In the Reference section at the back of this book I have listed many tools that will help you. Most important of all though is your own desire to heal. No prayer, essential oil, homeopathic remedy or flower remedy will help you if you cannot or will not forgive.

✦

PART V.

SUMMARY

Summary

It is my desire for the wounds of humanity to be healed. Helping each man and woman understand the totality of their decision-making process before they conceive a child is the only sensible choice, in my view, if we no longer want to face the continuing pain that comes from unwanted children or from children who do not reach full term.

If a child is indeed wanted, then all due care should be taken to provide a safe and healthy passage from the moment of conception, through birth, and into young adulthood. The family unit needs to be preserved and upheld with love. Love needs to be the ground from which the family springs. True love needs to be the primary imprint of what we create globally. Love is a Sacred resonance from the Creator Source and is centered in the heart.

Too many families have become broken through parental difficulties and divorce. The parents in these families often have not known love as children, so they have no basis upon which to build love in their relationship. Their hearts are wounded and not open in the way that hearts can be open when love is given freely from the moment of conception. As a result, the children of these wounded parents do not know true love either. They may witness bitter battles between their parents, which then become a relationship norm for them. This repeats from generation to generation, unless a conscious change can be made. Wounds between parents and children are often very similar for many generations. Where can the love and nurturing they so desperately need be found ? How can we expect the children born into these families to know how to make choices based on true love, respect and long-term commitments?

Choosing a partner carefully is not something that is taught in schools. Certainly the examples we see on television are not helpful. Sadly, the media primarily shows us lust and sensuality, rather than the true meaning of love. Love is the only thing that will bring a relationship into a state of grace.

Too many young people whose families are unhappy end up in a sexual relationship as a way of finding love. Sex for the sake of sex is not love. Building a relationship on sex alone will only bring unhappiness in the long run and, in many cases, unwanted children.

Many young teenage girls think that if they have a child that the child will love them, even if no one else does. Often the mother, who is a child herself, seeks love from boys or men who are incapable of being fathers in the truest sense of the word. Before long, the children from these unions are abandoned or abused as the young mother finds they are holding her back from the places she believes real love exists. Or perhaps the young mother ends up in a loveless marriage because of the child, which results in divorce. In these cases, another wounded child, who will struggle to find love is left alone, and the pattern is repeated.

The young mother may continue to seek love from other sources, still trying to fill the void inside that was created by her own parents' inability to express love and also, perhaps, from wounds in her past lives that blocked her ability to love.

Generations of wounded Souls can be enmeshed in this unhappy pattern. These situations do not only happen in places of poverty or illiteracy. Many wealthy families have loveless lives, using the leverage of money to buy false love and loyalties, and in some cases even encouraging their daughters to be in loveless marriages for social or financial gain.

In the end, over many years of loss and abandonment, with a trail of broken relationships and neglected children or abortions behind her, a woman may learn, if she is lucky, that the love she seeks is not outside of herself or in someone else but is rather a Divine state of awareness of the Creator within. She may finally understand that, until she learns to love herself and the Divine Source within her own Being, she cannot truly love another. Only then, can the real healing begin for her and for her children.

✦

Many religious families hide a plethora of sliding values within their group. I have witnessed more hatefulness and hidden violence in these families than in non-religious groups who are despised by these same pious groups. Something is sadly wrong where fear and indoctrination drive a woman to a secret abortion rather than facing the wrath of her family or her religion and the possibility of becoming an outcast.

+

I have seen grown men weep when they speak of abortions against their wishes that their wives or girlfriends have had.

I have seen women weep who were forced to have an abortion by the father of their child or who chose to end the pregnancy rather than bring a child into a violent marriage.

I have seen women deliberately imposing fatherhood upon men where the women alone made the decision to get pregnant. I have seen the damage in the children so conceived.

I have seen women damaged by rape and subsequent abortion.

I have seen parents, desperate to conceive, losing child after child to miscarriages due to poor nutrition and low progesterone in the woman.

I have seen the great devastation from all of these things, and the misery it creates in the human condition.

What a great sadness is here! The lack of communication and love is immense.

People are out of touch with their Inner Spirit and with the sanctity of life. They are therefore out of touch with each other and are unable to communicate in a sane way about children.

+

I have had clients come to me from all of the above groups with their stories of terror, grief and shame. Unless you have walked in another's shoes, you cannot possibly know what they have gone through. When you can begin to understand the whole picture, the whole dynamic behind a person's choices, then you will have compassion for them.

217

Our choice should be to teach with love and compassion, and to help heal the wounds at all levels in parents and children, so that new generations can come forward without the terrible damage we currently see.

Love is available from the Creator Source at all times. However, if our wounds are too great, we may be cut off from receiving that Source in full power. If our minds are full of anger, hatred or blaming others for our condition, we cannot easily heal the wounds that hold us back from our true Divinity. Hence, we need to forgive in order to heal. We cannot prepare our Souls for true healing if we continue to hold a grudge or any negative thought against others.

✦

Being angry with a woman who chooses abortion is certainly not the way to handle the situation. She has most likely been driven to that choice by the lack of love and support in her relationship or from her family. Those who make these women scapegoats should look carefully at the whole picture before taking any action. They should also look deeply into their own Souls before they judge. Hatred and anger are dark forces that will destroy any being harboring them.

Splitting the two sides of the abortion issue into a war of good versus evil is very dangerous. Love and compassion for any woman who finds herself in such a desperate place that she chooses abortion is the *only* appropriate response. It is important to understand why she feels she must take such an action. Help her. Ask her what her needs are and do not crush her further, as she is already crushed and in a fearful state of mind. I have never met a woman who has faced abortion without trepidation. Show her the prayers in this book. Let her see all sides of the situation. Let her know she can speak to the child's Spirit. Together, the mother, the father (if he is available and supportive) and the child's Spirit should be the ones who decide what is appropriate for them. It is not appropriate for anyone else to intrude upon this Sacred space unless the mother or father requests their help as a Spiritual counselor. The decision to have an abortion is one that will deeply affect the rest of their lives. In my view, it must be their informed decision alone. To force another person to your viewpoint is to take on their karma and become enmeshed with it. Not even the Angels are allowed to intervene in another's free will, thugh they may gently guide us. I believe that life is a unique path and journey for each individual. We are given free will. We create our own karma and are fully responsible for what we do.

I have had the opportunity to view many cases, including my own, and have seen how the power of the thoughts of the parents and others can affect the incoming child.

> *I caution all people who take a vicious stance against any woman choosing abortion to be aware. If they force her to bear the child, the child will most likely be damaged by the mother's fears and by their thoughts also. If the mother chooses abortion, the child will be burdened by the hatred of those who spoke against the woman, for whatever hatred is cast upon the mother also greatly affects the child. Thus, the child will be held back further from the Light by the words and actions of those who have negative thoughts about the situation.*

I have witnessed these wounds so many times and in so many situations. It is important to realize the power of negative thoughts and the damage they can do. You would probably be horrified to see what damage is done if you could see as I do.

> *Be mindful of your thoughts. Make them of love.*

The only way that I know to help this world is to have compassion and to rise above the immediate scene to a higher view in order to see what has really taken place. If you are not able or willing to see these things, then I caution you to refrain from judging another's position. Love, compassion and forgiveness are the only way.

> I have seen the wounds of mothers who were forced to give their children up for adoption.
>
> I have seen the wounds of adopted children who can never rest because they do not know why they were given up for adoption.
>
> I have seen the wounds of children who miscarried when a parent did not want them.

I have seen the wounds of parents who truly wanted a child that miscarried due to exposure to toxic substances in the environment.

I have seen the wounds of stillborn children who wanted to live, but could not, due to a body that was distorted from the mother ingesting contaminated food and water, or by inoculations given to one or both of the parents.

I have seen the wounds of parents still grieving for their stillborn child thirty years after.

I have seen the wounds and illnesses of women who have had abortions, whose bodies continue to weep and cry out for completion.

I have seen the wounds of aborted children who are broken hearted and angry that they were cast out.

I have seen how so many children who died before their time have never reached the Light, and that they urgently need our help.

Over the years, I have seen more than most people would ever want to see. For this reason, I ask you to resolve any anger and to call love into your heart. Not one of the men, women or children in these stories wanted to be in the place they found themselves. Not one of them has forgotten the sad events in their lives. Will you love them and help them? Will you help humanity rise beyond his great sadness? Will you stand for global peace and harmony?

> *My prayer is that you will forgive all humanity and help with the prayers of transition and that you will understand that the principles given here are the principles of Love. Please share this book with others and let it be known that there is another way: it is the way of Love, Compassion and Forgiveness. It is the way that all the great teachers have taught.*

> *May the Angels bless you and walk with you on your path as you bring healing grace to the world.*

✦

AFTERWORD

Journey to the Moment of Conception

After writing this book, I realized I still wanted to know more. The question of when the Spirit enters the body is one that many have argued over for centuries. It spurred me on to deeper research within my own Being. I knew my parents had planned my birth and that I had willingly come to them. I also knew that my mother and I had experienced good past lives together and that I looked forward to being with both my parents. I had been visiting with them in Spirit for months before conception took place, listening to their thoughts and dreams, and I knew they wanted a little girl.

✢

Now, fifty years later, I wanted to remember my Spiritual journey at the very beginning of this present incarnation. So, in meditation, I asked my Angels to help me go back to that first moment just before the sperm met the egg.

I found myself in Spirit, deep in the void, far from the Earth's physical sphere floating timelessly in grace, awaiting the moment to arrive. It was peaceful, yet there was an expectancy in the moment, knowing that my time was coming soon to re-enter the physical world. I had been in communion with my Guides and Teachers about the events to come, and now I was in a deep state of consciousness. I was very much aware of the Presence of the Source all around me, of an All-Knowing Consciousness within the Un-Manifest Light of which I was a part.

Then, as sperm united with egg in the physical world, the non-physical world seemed to erupt around me. It was as though a sonic boom had rippled through all space and time. The universe seemed to be aware of the new life just beginning to be formed, as though it registered within each

223

sentient Being at Spirit level. The web of life vibrated and shimmered throughout the cosmos. My Spirit was fully aware of the cosmic union between the two bright life streams that was taking place. These two intertwining energies were forming a spiraling vortex of Light through which I was being drawn at lightning speed. I found myself hurtling through space-time into the physical plane of the Earthly existence. The Source knew it all and watched and guided me. Nothing could have stopped me from responding to that immense magnetic pull into the physical world. It was with a feeling of exhilaration and joy that I returned. My Spirit entered into the tiny fertilized egg in a flash of Light. It felt as though I had entered into a cosmos of spinning Light. Perhaps this was the DNA of my father and mother combining within that first cell. It was a magical dancing Light with all the sounds, colors and music of the cosmos within it. My heart at Spirit level became one with the tiny fertilized egg. This was the first moment of my Becoming in this present incarnation. There was no other moment so deafening, so enthralling as that explosion in the deep fields of space. From that time on my Spiritual heart was connected to, and very much a part of, the small fertilized egg that would become my Physical Body. The very essence of my Being was centered upon that small beginning, yet as I watched, it seemed that the egg held all the potential of the cosmos within it also. This was of cosmic proportions at one level, and yet so minute on the physical level.

✦

As I watched in my meditation, I saw my small body grow from egg, to embryo, to fetus, and to final birth. There was not one moment that I was not able to see. It was all recorded deep in my Spiritual and cellular memory, but until now I had not tried to access it consciously.

In the first few months, I felt the sadness and aloneness of my mother, being so far away from her own mother. Then, I felt the disapproval and irritation of her mother as she traveled four hundreds miles across England to help before my birth. I felt the sweetness of my two-year old brother turn to pain and anguish as he was taken to the hospital for surgery just before I was born. I felt his great upset after he returned, not wanting me to be born, because he desperately needed our parents' love after feeling abandoned in the hospital. I felt the crushing suffocation of being born. Then the crispness against my cheek of the nurse's white uniform up against me as she put iodine in my eyes. There was stinging, and blurriness, and the smells of antiseptic and starched linen. Then I was finally being placed into my mother's arms and I nestled up against her breasts with her familiar smell. It was all so very real and so very much embedded in my memory.

✦

Now, I can never doubt when the Spirit is connected. No matter how early the pregnancy, even if no visible heart is yet beating, the Spirit of the child is strongly attached. It is the Spirit's own conscious heart energy, connected to the Source, which forms the focus for the physical heart and body. It is this energy that is the motivating power behind cell division and without the first cell dividing, no heart or body could develop. The body of the incoming Spirit is Sacred, no matter how small.

When I asked myself, as I watched in meditation that tender moment of Becoming, how I would have felt if someone had thought to abort me, I felt a huge pain in my heart. It seemed as though my heart would have been torn in two. This, thank God, was *not* something my mother had ever thought about, but now I know for sure how it must feel when abortion is considered. The Spiritual heart is the connection through which the Spirit over-lights, and communicates with, the child's growing body. A child cannot be considered non-human even in its earliest stage of growth. He or she is a Spiritual Being, a very precious gift from God.

✦

We must nurture the children of the Earth, whoever they are, and we must nurture each other. It is our destiny to become Christed Beings, at peace with each other and at One with God, while still in the Physical Body. We are all holders of the Light of the Creator within our Spiritual hearts. This is how we began our journey. It is now time for us all to awaken to our inner glory.

✦

REFERENCE
SECTION

Reference Section

INFORMATION ON HORMONE HEALTH:

Progesterone balance is essential for carrying a child full term and to balance hormones after the loss of a child. Low progesterone can lead to cancer.

These excellent books and tapes by John R. Lee, M.D., will help you understand hormone health:

The Invisible Hormone, Progesterone's Role in 20th Century Diseases.
By John R. Lee, M.D., This is a two-cassette tape set.

What Your Doctor May Not Tell You About Menopause:
The Breakthrough Book On Natural Progesterone.
By John R. Lee, M.D., with Virginia Hopkins.
ISBN 0-446-67144-4

What Your Doctor May Not Tell You About Premenopause: Balance Your Hormones and Your Life From Thirty to Fifty.
By John R. Lee, M.D., Jesse Hanley, M.D., and Virginia Hopkins.
ISBN 0-446-67380-3

What Your Doctor May Not Tell You About Breast Cancer: How Hormone Balance Can Help Save Your Life.
By John R. Lee, MD, David Zava, Ph.D., and Virginia Hopkins.
ISBN 0-446-52686-X

SPIRITUAL READING:

The Angels' Guide Book to Living on Earth.
By Gwendolyn Awen Jones.

Explains the Prayer of Light in depth. Order information at the back of this book on page 239.

The Angels' Guide to Forgiveness.
By Gwendolyn Awen Jones

Explains the Forgiveness Prayer in depth. Order information at the back of this book on page 239.

The Isaiah Effect. Decoding the Lost Science of Prayer and Prophecy.
By Gregg Braden.
ISBN 0-609-80796-X

This book explains the lost science behind prayer and documents which books were removed from the Bible in the fourth century AD. An important read.

Cosmic Cradle. Souls Waiting in the Wings for Birth.
By Elizabeth M. Carmen and Neil J. Carmen Ph.D.
ISBN 1-887472-71-1

An uplifting book of communications between parents and children before birth.

Feelings Buried Alive Never Die.
by Karol K.Truman.
Published by Oympus Distributing,
P.O. Box 4218, St. George, Utah   84771
ISBN 0911207-02-3

An excellent book that will help you understand how to resolve negative feelings and how feelings affect your health.

The Biology of Transcendence. A Blueprint of the Human Spirit.
By Joseph Chilton Pearce.
ISBN 0-89281-990-1

This is a wonderful book that parallels my own research using scientific method. An illuminating description of how the brain develops in the fetus and growing child.

The Body Electric. Electromagnetism and the Foundation of Life.
By Robert O. Becker, M.D., and Gary Sheldon.
ISBN 0-688-06971-1

This book explains how our body functions and how even small electromagnetic fields can damage cell growth. Essential reading for women who are pregnant and for all people using computers and cell phones.

Fast Food Nation. The Dark Side of the All American Meal.
By Eric Schlosser.
ISNB 0-06-093845-5

To grow a healthy child you need healthy food. Fast food does not support health. This book exposes the truth behind fast food and empty calories.

HOMEOPATHY:

Emotional Healing with Homeopathy. **(The new 2003 edition)**
By Peter Chappell BSc. RSHom. FSHom.
Available from www.homeopathic.com

This is an excellent resource. It explains how to use homeopathic remedies for trauma and emotional problems. Staphysagira (also spelled Staphisagria) and its use is detailed fully for those who have had a hysterectomy or an abortion. Stramonium use is explained for those who have faced severe, physical violence (such as during a rape). It should be used *before* using the Staphysagria remedy, to remove the effects of violent trauma. Homeopathics range in strength. Low potencies of 6C to 30C are available in health stores. The potency given to me was the strongest, LM1, and is only available through your homeopath or by direct order from a homoepathic supplier. I encourage you to read Chappell's book for correct usage and share it with your local homeopath, as not all are aware of his important research on emotional healing. Chappell teaches homeopathy widely throughout Europe.
For homeopathic supplies and practitioners in your area visit www. homeopathichome.com

For homeopathic supplies by phone, this is the source I have used:
Hahneman Laboratories Inc.
1-888-427-6422

ESSENTIAL OILS:

Please be sure to only use *pure therapeutic-grade* essential oils for healing work. Cheaper oils can be found but may not be pure, may not have the same benefits and could even cause problems if they are cut with toxic fillers.

When I first used pure therapeutic grade essential oils, I was amazed at the difference compared to lower grades available in general stores. I found that therapeutic grade oils will change the auric field dramatically, brightening it up rapidly and will help release negative emotional patterns. Cheaper, low grade oils will not do this, so be sure to use a source that is certified therapeutic grade. Find a good aromatherapy practitioner to help you make the right choices. The blends mentioned in this book are as follows:

1. For courage and valor before dealing with difficult situations: I use a blend of rosewood, blue tansy, frankincense and spruce in a carrier of almond oil.

2. For strengthening the auric field, (the special blend I call the essence of the Angels): I use ylang ylang, rose, melissa, sandalwood, geranium, spruce, myrrh, hyssop, bergamot and rosewood in a carrier of almond oil.

3. For releasing negative emotions: I use a blend of ylang ylang, lavandin, geranium, sandalwood, and blue tansy in a carrier of olive oil.

4. For general protection, healing and Spiritual prayer work I use Frankincense.

For links to information on therapeutic-grade essential oils go to my website: **www.angelsoflightandhealing.org**

Essential Science Publishing has many books, videos and tapes that may help you learn how to use essential oils. They also carry a good range of books, on other healing modalities.

Visit them on the web at **www.essentialscience.net**

Essential Science Publishing : 1-800-336-6308

BACH FLOWER REMEDIES:

The Bach Flower Remedies, Step by Step. A Complete Guide to Selecting and Using the Remedies.
By Judy Howard
ISBN 0-85207-223-6

This book will give you all the information on how to use these gentle remedies. A few drops in a glass of water, sipped throughout the day is the way to use them.

"Rescue Remedy" will help you after any shock or trauma. "Star of Bethlehem" will help you handle loss. There are a total of thirty-eight remedies and will be found in any good health food store.

ANTI-DEPRESSANTS:

Prozac, Panacea or Pandora?
By Ann Blake Tracy, Ph.D.
Cassia Publications, P.O.Box 1044, West Jordan, UT 84084
1-800-280-0730

Dr. Ann Blake Tracy has done an in-depth study of the effects of all SSRI (Specific Serotonin Reuptake Inhibitors) antidepressants. This information is very disturbing on how it affects the fetus and the user of these drugs. She has made an important tape to help a person safely withdraw from this drug use. If you are using Prozac, Zoloft, Paxil, Lovan, Luvox or any other drug in this class, I strongly recommend you research this information and avoid pregnancy while taking the drugs. Dr.Blake's website will give you up to date information on these drugs: **www.drugawareness.org**

ADOPTION:

The Other Mother : A True Story - A woman's love for the child she gave up for adoption.
By Carol Schaefer
ISBN 0-939149-75-3

This is an important book that describes in detail the adoption process. A true life story that should be read before anyone considers giving up a child for adoption. Under pressure as a pregnant teenager, Carol surrendered her baby for adoption. It devastated her emotionally. She never forgot her child and knew intuitively what was happening to him in his life as he grew. When the legal process allowed her to search for him 19 years later she was finally able to see him again and come to know his other mother as a good friend. The book includes valuable resources in the appendix to help birth parents find the children they have given up for adoption.

GLOSSARY

GLOSSARY

As I have used terms in this book that others may use differently, I have included this glossary to help you understand my meaning.

✦

Astral Body: the dream body that can go into the realms of Light during sleep. It has a human form but is made out of a finer substance of Light.

Chakras: Spinning vortices of Light. They are part of the body's energy system that draw in life force and energize the Physical Body. There are seven major chakras or energy centers on the Physical Body and several minor ones.

Christ: Jesus the Christ. Jesus was able to *consciously* become One with the heart resonance of the Creator. This is the Christ energy of Divine Love. We can all become One with the Christ resonance of Divine Love as Jesus did by realizing Oneness with the Creator Source in our hearts. We can then bring the Christ Light of healing into our own Being and help others. I use the term Christ to mean the Spiritual Master Jesus, in His Christed Awareness.

Christ Light: This is the Light of Love that comes directly from the Source. It is the most exquisite energy and can heal all things. It generally has a bright golden color. See Light.

Christed: This is when a person at heart level becomes fully conscious of, and fully illuminated by, the Light and Love of God. It is our destiny to become Christed or fully awakened while in the Physical Body. Jesus

235

became a Christed person and can act an intermediary for those who wish to reach Christ Consciousness. The Christ energy is of the highest form of Love. However, one does not have to be of the Christian faith to become One with God or become Christed. Any tradition that links a person to the Heart of the Creator Source and Divine Love will help that person to become Christed. All people are a part of the One Source. Becoming conscious of that connection is the key to enlightenment.

Emotional Body: This is our feeling body through which we sense and know things about our environment. It is an egg-shaped body of Light and depending upon the health of a person may extend three to five feet around the Physical Body. The Emotional Body can have a tremendous influence upon the health of a person. Positive feelings will help this body heal; negative ones will make it dark, creating illness.

Entity: A discarnate Being who has not yet gone into the Light, not to be confused with your Angels, Guides and Teachers, who are not in a Physical Body but are operating in their Spiritual Bodies to help you. I use the term Entity to mean a Being in a less advanced sate of awareness that is without a Physical Body and who has not chosen to go into the Light, or who is stuck between the realms. Entities can be of human origin but are not necessarily so. Some Entities are not ready for the Light and choose to live in a darkened place; they are going through their own evolutionary cycle.

Etheric Body: This body is made up of a network of Light that surrounds and penetrates our Being. This matrix of Light carries our life energy to the cells. If this matrix is broken, the cells can no longer receive energy and will begin to die. Re-establishing the Etheric Body network of Light is essential for health especially after surgery.

God: Father-Mother-God, Source, Creator, are all the same in my text and represent the essential underlying, creative, loving, energy behind all Creation.

Higher Self: Spirit. This is the Spiritual aspect of a person, his connection to God. It is the conduit through which the energy of the Source comes. If the connection between the Spirit and the Soul is damaged for any reason, then the life force of that person will be weak. In a Spiritually advanced person the Higher Self or Spirit will show as a bright radiance around the whole Being.

Inner Child: At conception, the Spirit sends a small part of its total Being into incarnation with the information that is needed for the development of the life mission. This is the seed energy for the new child, which I call the Inner Child. It is around the Spiritual Essence of the Inner Child that all levels of the newly incarnating Being are coalesced. The mission for life is encoded within the Inner Child and is centered in the heart. For perfect health the Inner Child needs to stay in full contact with its Higher Self or Spirit, for life to be flowing well. If trauma occurs in gestation or childhood, the Inner Child may lose its Spiritual direction and the person may lose the sense of Self.

Inner Plane: This refers to the all the dimensions beyond the physical senses. There are many levels to the Inner Plane all operating on different frequencies. Most people will never notice what is around them on these other levels. This is probably for the best, as they would most likely have a sensory overload, if they were not trained for it. Staying within well-known Spiritual pathways, using prayer and meditation, is the best way to navigate through the many levels of the Inner Plane.

Karma: Karma can be good or bad depending upon our actions in past lives, and our aspirations in this life. Our Spiritual journey to full enlightenment requires us to clear our negative energy from the past. The Soul desires to return to a state of Grace and Love. In order to do so it is drawn back to places and people to clear difficulties with them. Negative karma can most often be cleared with prayer work and forgiveness to release the entanglements between the Soul and others.

Light: If this word has a capital letter in my text I am referring to the Christ Light, the Light of Love, that lies beyond the normal physical senses and not to regular daylight. Going into the Light is simply shifting consciousness to the level of the Creator's Divine Love, where all illusion of illness and death is healed. At this highest Spiritual level there is Divine Health, but as the Spirit comes into incarnation, there are many lower energies to contend with on the Earth Plane, including karma carried by the Soul from past lives that can impede the Light as it enters the Physical Being. Remembering the true perfection of the Spiritual Being allows the Light to dissolve away the illusion of illness.

Mental Body: The Mental Body extends beyond the Physical and Emotional Bodies, and is a finer, subtler energy field. It is the body of our creative thinking and can be easily distorted by negative thinking. Positive thinking, prayer and meditation on the Light of God will help clear the Mental Body of negativity.

Physical Body: This is the flesh and blood body of the physical plane, which is the outward expression of all the other levels of consciousness of the incarnating Being.

Reincarnation: Refers to the Soul's continuing journey through many lifetimes taking a on different Physical Body each lifetime.

Soul: The Soul holds the memories of all previous incarnations within its matrix, which can affect the Physical Body's development. The Soul can be young or very old. Old Souls have often been on Earth many lifetimes and have had time to clear their karma. They are witnessed by their Love and Compassion for Humanity. Young Souls may often be very involved with material wants and desires. The Soul is a creation of the Spirit, which over-lights the Soul at all times. However the Soul can be cut off from the memory of its Spiritual aspect by sudden traumatic death, violent acts against it, drugs, alcohol and certain dogmatic belief systems that instill fear of God instead of Love. The Soul should have a bright golden energy but is often depleted by negativity from events in this life and past lives.

Spirit: See Higher Self. The Spirit is the creation of God, an individualized aspect of the Divine Creator Source. It is the highest level of the human energy field.

Thought Form: Created by the Mental Body and energized by the Emotional Body, a thought form can act upon the Physical Body in a negative or positive way, depending upon what the original intention of the person was who created it. Negative thought forms can be dissolved away with Christ Light and prayer work.

✦

OTHER BOOKS
BY THE AUTHOR

The Angels' Guide Book to Living on Earth.
By Gwendolyn Awen Jones.

Explains the Prayer of Light in depth. $10.00 + S & H $2.50

The Angels' Guide to Forgiveness.
By Gwendolyn Awen Jones

Explains the Forgiveness Prayer in depth. $10.00 + S & H $2.50

A Cry from the Womb: Healing the Heart of the World.
By Gwendolyn Awen Jones.

Deluxe Limited Edition, numbered and signed by the author.
Only 1,000 copies printed. $100.00 + S & H $5.00

A Cry from the Womb: Healing the Heart of the World.
By Gwendolyn Awen Jones.

Paperback edition. $18.95 + S & H $5.00

Sales tax : Please add 8.25% for orders shipped to Texas.

Please send checks payable to Gwendolyn Awen Jones.
Angels of Light and Healing,
P.O. Box 311448, New Braunfels, TX 78131-1448

For upcoming events, lectures and new books by Gwendolyn
Awen Jones, visit the website: www.angelsoflightandhealing.org

CPSIA information can be obtained at www.ICGtesting.com
Printed in the USA
LVOW051936310812

296785LV00002B/204/A